"My Friends"

Bob Jones

BOB JONES UNIVERSITY PRESS
Greenville, South Carolina 29614

"My friends"
by Bob Jones Sr.
©1983 Bob Jones University Press
Greenville, South Carolina 29614
ISBN 0-89084-230-2
All rights reserved
Printed in the United States of America

Contents

7 Some people say you cannot prove that there is a God. Well you can. I've proved it. If there's ever been one prayer answered in the history of the world, that's all the proof you need that there's a God.

13 When there is a good, straight road to the place you should go, why go a roundabout way to get there?

21 Help from man is not really help unless God sends it through man.

27 The Christian philosophy is a philosophy of self-denial and self-control; the satanic philosophy is a philosophy of "do as you please, live your own life."

35 The most important light in your home is not the chandelier in the parlor. It's that little back hall light.

43 A man without enemies is a man who has accomplished nothing. You cannot move without producing friction.

49 A man whose supreme desire is to do what is right has no difficulty finding out what is right.

57 There is no tragedy as tragic as combining high mentality with low morality.

63 It is never right to do something wrong, even to get an opportunity to do something that is right.

69 Heaven and Hell are in opposite directions, and no man can travel both ways at the same time.

75 You do what you ought not to do, because you do not do what you ought to do.

83 No man is high born until he is born from on high.

89 God is the same person yesterday, today, and forever; but in the drama of the ages He plays many parts.

95 Your character is what God knows you to be; your reputation is what men think you are.

101 A Christian does good deeds, but doing good deeds does not make a man a Christian.

107 An illiterate person is one who cannot tell you what he knows; an ignorant person is one who does not know anything to tell you.

113 Life is not divided into the secular and the sacred. For a Christian, everything is sacred.

121 God will not do for you what He gives you strength to do for yourself.

127 The wise man prepares for the inevitable.

Preface

"My friends..." What an appropriate title for a collection of radio messages by Dr. Bob Jones, Sr.! Having been connected with the BJU radio station for many years, it was my privilege to be on hand for just about every one of Dr. Jones's early morning radio broadcasts. His style for these radio talks was quite different from the style he used in his sermons from the pulpit or the chapel platform where he was always forceful, often fiery, and even bombastic in the very best sense of the word. In the radio studios, he was conversational, warm, and friendly. Those listening at their radios at home had the distinct feeling that they were sitting across from Dr. Jones at a table or desk, listening to him chat.

He was no less forceful than in the pulpit or on the chapel platform, but his style was perfectly adapted for the more intimate medium of radio. The very opening words, "My friends," were themselves disarming.

This aspect of Dr. Jones's radio ministry can be illustrated by a touching incident that took place just a few years after the radio station went on the air. We had been hearing regularly from a lady who was blind and bedfast with crippling arthritis. Her letters had to be dictated through her mother since her hands were so terribly crippled.

Some of us from the radio station visited her from time to time, and on one of these visits, just as we were leaving, the lady said, "When you get back to the school, you tell Dr. Bob how much we appreciate him coming into our home each morning and visiting with us." What more touching tribute could be made to the radio ministry of this man?

For those of us who have been with the University for many years and benefited almost daily from the commonsense, hard-as-nails, but thoroughly biblical philosophy of Dr. Bob Jones, Sr., it is hard to realize that almost a generation of students and even some faculty members have grown up who never knew him personally. Certainly, never before in our history was this solidly Christian philosophy of life so greatly needed as it is today. This book, which is taken almost verbatim from a series of radio talks based on the sayings for which he was so famous, will go a long way toward preserving for the present and future generations the Christian philosophy of Dr. Bob Jones, Sr.

"My friends . . ." please do read on through this entire book.

—*James Ryerson*

"Some people say you cannot prove that there is a God. Well you can. I've proved it. If there's ever been one prayer answered in the history of the world, that's all the proof you need that there's a God."

My friends, as I've gone up and down the world preaching the Gospel, I've had people to come to me who thought they were very smart and they've said to me, "You cannot prove there's a God." I always tell them you can. I have. I've proved there's a God. If I've ever had a prayer answered, that's all the proof I need that there is a God.

Suppose I wake up in the night and it's dark in my room and I say, "I'm very hungry. I'd like to have something to eat." I reach out in the darkness and get a sandwich in my hand. I can't see anybody and really don't feel anybody especially, but I reach my hand out and there's a sandwich, and I eat this sandwich and my hunger's satisfied. I go to bed the next night and wake up about 2 o'clock in the morning. It's dark, and I say, "I'm thirsty. I'd like to have a drink of water." And I reach my hand out in the dark and

"My friends"

get a glass of water and drink it. I'm not a fool. I soon decide there's somebody around there somewhere that knows when a fellow needs something. I've never seen God literally, but you know, many times when it's been dark, I've asked God for some things and gotten them. I *know* there is a God.

Suppose I'm going along the road, and my shoulders are weighed down by a heavy burden, and I look up in the sky, and I say, "God, You're up there somewhere. I know You're there because 'the fool hath said in his heart, There is no God,' and I know You're up there. My mind tells me You're there. But You know, I'm awfully tired. This load I'm carrying is just a little more than I can carry by myself. I'd like to have some rest." I've done that many times, and you know, I didn't see God's arms when they came down, but I sure did feel Him lift the load.

And sometimes I've come to where the road parted, and I have stood there and said, "I don't know which way to go." And I've looked up. I've said, "God, You know the right road for a fellow to take. And here I am, I've got to go one way or the other, I've got to move right now, please show me." And somehow I've managed to find the road. Don't tell *me* there's no God.

You know, God is very real to some of us. If He isn't real to you, He can be. We tell our students in Bob Jones University that there's a real God in this universe. A *real* God. God is not some personality so far away that man cannot touch Him.

There is a God

I don't know what people do without God. How do they live without fellowship with Him? You get in trouble, you can go jump in the river if you want to. But I have another place to go: a little corner in the room, where I simply sit down and talk to God.

Do you know God? If you do not, you don't know anything worth knowing. You can know a great many things *about* God and never know God. You can know a good deal about science and never know the God of the universe. You can go to a scientific laboratory and stay there day after day and never find God. Man by searching cannot find God.

How can you find Him? You poor little weak finite creature; you can't find God. But if you want God to, He can surely find you. The picture in the Bible is not a picture of a sheep looking for a shepherd; it's the picture of the shepherd looking for his sheep. It's not the picture of a lost coin looking for the owner, it's the owner looking for the lost coin. The whole picture of God in the Bible is a picture of God going out and looking for people. "Tell them to come to Me, come to Me," He says. "Come to Me all the ends of the earth. Come to Me and be ye saved."

At Bob Jones University our academic standards are high, and we're going to keep them high. We exalt God Almighty here, but we don't lower any legitimate standards. When we put God first, every standard that's decent goes up, too. In all things He's to have the preeminence, and that puts up everything else, puts up the standards of love and the standards of family life and the standards of business life. But we tell our students if they stay here and make a brilliant record, make A's and graduate and go out and have no God-consciousness, we'll consider them failures. There are more important things than making A's in universities—the most important thing is for a man to fear God and know God.

We read in the Bible, "The fear of the Lord is the beginning of knowledge" (Proverbs 1:7), and that means it's the *chief part* of knowledge; the fear of God is the main thing in knowledge. Not cowardly fear; not that kind of fear. Not a hysterical excitement—not that. It's a holy reverence and sense of awe in the presence of the infinite God.

It's more important for you to know the God who made the universe than it is to understand the universe. You can measure the distance between stars, and you can talk about how long it takes a ray of light to come from a distant sun to this earth and figure it out accurately. That sounds so wonderful, but it is more important to know that out yonder somewhere there is a God, and that this God struck a match on the rock of His omnipotence and lighted the world from which that ray of light is coming to this earth. Do you know God? The elements of bread are everywhere about us, but we can't eat those elements until we get them in a loaf. Now, the Bible makes it plain that God is omnipresent; God is everywhere in the universe; He fills all space; eternity is His home. There wasn't any other house big

There is a God

enough to hold Him but eternity—He inhabits it. Jesus Christ was God fixed up in the form of a man walking around in this world—God incarnate. He was God fixed up so poor, hungry hearts can feed on the Bread that came down from Heaven. It's so real. I wonder why you folks won't let God be real to you.

Suppose God should suddenly die on the throne of the universe. Of course, He's not going to die; but suppose He should? Suppose while I'm talking, God should die and the angels should have a conference and say, "Somebody ought to go down yonder and tell somebody listening to Bob Jones that God is dead." I wonder if you'd know it before the angels came. Would you know it before a committee flew down from Heaven to earth to tell you? Some of us wouldn't know it. We'd say, "What's the matter? It's dark. The stars are all dead. It's night; I'm lonely. Where is God?" Do you know God? You can know Him. You can know Him by accepting Jesus Christ, His Son, as your Saviour. Yield yourself to Him and trust Him as your personal Saviour and dedicate your life to Him and be what you ought to be and live in fellowship with Him. For the Bible makes it plain, "If we walk in the light, as he is in the light, we have fellowship one with another, and the blood of Jesus Christ his Son cleanseth us from all sin" (I John 1:7).

Our Heavenly Father, bless all who read this today, and bless Bob Jones University. And until all the things of this world end and until Jesus comes back again, help Bob Jones University to

"My friends"

continue to put the emphasis here: God first, knowing God—the chief part of knowledge. And help us never to forget that to know God is worth more than anything else. And may someone, after hearing this message, come to know Him. We pray in the wonderful name of Jesus Christ our Lord. Amen.

"When there is a good, straight road to the place you should go, why go a roundabout way to get there?"

My friends, I am constantly meeting people who say to me, "I cannot understand the Bible. There are so many things I can't understand." Well, I usually ask them to tell me something they *can* understand. And they usually find something that's very simple, and they say, "That's clear." And I say to them, "Live up to that."

One time a man went to a preacher and said, "I don't understand the Bible."

"Well," the preacher said, "let's see how much you *can* understand. We'll start with the Ten Commandments. Now, take this one, 'Thou shalt not steal' " (Exodus 20:15).

"What does the Bible say about stealing?"

"Well, it says, 'Thou shalt not steal.' That's clear, isn't it?"

"Yes."

"Well, why don't you quit stealing?"

"My friends"

"Oh," he said, "I understand that."

You know the fundamental statements of the Bible are perfectly clear. There never has been any book like the Bible. It's simple, and clear, and full of meaning if you have a spiritual and understanding mind. There may be things in the Bible that are too deep for you and too high for you—things that you never can quite grasp. But all the essential things are stated very simply. Take this statement, "I am the way, the truth, and the life" (John 14:6). That's clear, isn't it? What does that mean?

Jesus said, "You want to go to Heaven, don't you?"

"Yes."

"Well, I am the Way."

"You're the Way?"

"Yes, I am the Way."

"You mean I've got to go to Heaven by You?"

"Yes, I am the Way."

That's simple.

Now take another passage, "For God so loved the world, that he gave his only begotten Son, that whosoever believeth in him should not perish, but have everlasting life" (John 3:16). What does that mean? God gave Jesus, and Jesus died on the cross. So if a man would believe in Him, he would not perish but have everlasting life. That's not hard to understand.

Take another passage—it's so clear and simple: "For by grace are ye saved through faith; and that not of yourselves; it is the gift of God" (Ephesians 2:8). By grace through faith. What is

Take the straight road

grace? Grace is something you don't earn. That means that you can't earn salvation. You can't pay for it after you get it. It's something that you can't earn that's given to you by God. By grace are ye saved. That means you're saved by the mercy and kindness and goodness and graciousness of God. Now, how are you saved? Through faith. Through faith. What is faith? It's believing something. Faith in the Bible means just exactly what faith means in the dictionary. What does it mean in the dictionary? It means to believe something. That's all faith is. You believe something so firmly you commit yourself to it. "Believe on the Lord Jesus Christ, and thou shalt be saved" (Acts 16:31). That ought not to be hard. What's it mean to "believe on the Lord Jesus Christ?" Well, here's a man who is in jail. He's behind bars and he can't get out. He doesn't know what to do.

But he says to somebody, "I'd like to have a good lawyer. Who is a good lawyer?"

And they say, "So-and-So down here is a good lawyer."

"May I see him? Will you get him for me?"

And the lawyer comes and says, "What do you want?"

He says, "I want you to take my case. I don't know how to get out of jail. I need somebody who can get me out of this trouble. I put my case in your hands. You're the lawyer, and I'm willing to make a deal with you. I'll do what you say."

"All right," he says. "Don't say anything. Just leave it to me."

"My friends"

Now, what did that man do? He believed in the lawyer so much, he put his case in the lawyer's hands.

Here's a fellow who's sick and in a bad fix. He says, "I've tried everything I know to try. I've taken medicine. I've done the best I could. I don't know what to do with myself." He sends for a doctor. The doctor comes, and the fellow says, "Doctor, I'm sick. I want you to take my case. I just put myself in your hands." That's what it means to believe in Jesus Christ.

The greatest truths in the world are simple truths. As a matter of fact, simplicity is truth's most becoming garb. Oh, I've heard those preachers who stood up to speak and nobody knew what they were talking about. Why don't they come down to earth and talk so folks know what they're saying? I never have understood those people.

When Jesus was on the mountaintop, the Bible says the common people heard Him gladly. He talked so that the average, ordinary man could understand Him. The common people heard Him gladly. They said, "Never man spake like this man" (John 7:46). And they'd gather around Him. And little babies would try to get to Him, and plain women would hold up their little babies, and the little babies would stretch out their arms to get to Him.

The Sermon on the Mount has the most profound, philosophical statement ever uttered in one verse. "Blessed are the pure in heart: for they shall see God" (Matthew 5:8). Every word in that statement is a monosyllable, except one. "Blessed are the pure in heart: for they shall see God." There's never been a philosopher in the world who ever uttered a statement as profound as that. Think of it! Christ sat there on the mountaintop, with His disciples around Him, giving the most profound truths the world has ever heard in monosyllables.

I don't know what's the matter with us preachers. I don't know what's the matter with us Christians. Why don't we come down to earth where people live? I heard a preacher not long ago who talked, and talked, and talked. He was a great theologian and so profound. But all he said he could have said in three minutes, and everybody would have understood it.

Now, I don't take any stock in cutting sermons down *too* short. And I have no patience with the tendency in this day and time to put the Gospel train on a side track to let every horn-tooting train pass. I believe in preaching—old-time preaching. There are other things to preaching than just proclaiming the Gospel, because when Paul wrote Timothy, he told Timothy to "reprove" (it takes time for that), "rebuke" (it takes time for that), and told him to do it "with all longsuffering and doctrine" (II Timothy 4:2). I don't mean that a sermon necessarily has to be just a 15-minute sermon. If a man's on fire with the Holy Spirit, he'll stand up there if his heart is burning, and he won't have any trouble holding a crowd for a reasonable length of time. But when it comes to a point

"My friends"

of stating things so people can get hold of them, why not come to the point? Why go a roundabout road when there's a straight line there?

One time, a young fellow in a university went to a professor. He said, "Professor, I believe I could write a book of proverbs as wonderful as the Proverbs in the Bible."

He said, "All right, I'll tell you what you do. You just go write one; try it. Come back and see me in a day or two."

In a day or two he came back and said, "I can't write like that."

You *can't* write like that. God's truth is so simply clothed.

Now there are things in the Bible we can't understand. But if you are lost, if you are never saved, and if you don't go to Heaven when you die, it will not be because the road isn't well-marked. There are ten thousand voices in the world today clamoring to be heard. Somebody says do this, do that, or do the other. And I look up and say, "Jesus, they're all talking a great deal. Won't you tell me, please, Jesus, I'd like to know a way home." And Jesus says, "Why, I'm glad to tell you. I am the Way." "He that hath the Son hath life; and he that hath not the Son of God hath not life" (I John 5:12). If you have Christ, you have life; if you have Christ, you are a Christian. If you haven't Christ you haven't life; if you haven't Christ, you are not a Christian. "As many as received him, to them gave he power to become the sons of God, even to them that believe on his name" (John 1:12).

Take the straight road

Why don't you trust Him? Why do you go on and talk so much about the thing and say you can't understand? Just start right here and tell Jesus, "There's so much I don't know, but I believe you love me, and I believe you died for me, and I believe that You're able to save me. I'll trust You." If you'll do that, some day we'll be seeing each other. When the mists have rolled away over on the other side, we'll be at home together.

Our Father, we dedicate our lives anew to this simple statement of the Gospel truth, "Jesus died for us. He arose from the dead. He ascended into Heaven. We are saved by faith in His atoning blood which was shed on Calvary's cross." Keep us faithful and true, we pray in His name. Amen.

"Help from man is not really help unless God sends it through man."

My friends, the older I get, the more appreciation I have for the old-time practical Christian philosophy of the people I knew when I was a boy—my country father, my mother, and the neighbors who lived in the community. We didn't have as many books and as many schools, and we may not have known as much as some people know today, but we *did* have time to think things through. Out in the country, we used to have a way of saying, "By the help of God, I think I can do it."

But we've outgrown those days to a great extent, and now everybody's looking for help somewhere else. The psalmist said, "I will lift up mine eyes unto the hills, from whence cometh my help" (Psalm 121:1). You'll be interested to know (if you don't know it already) that that's in the form of a question. The psalmist says, "I will lift up mine eyes unto the hills. From whence cometh my help?" In other words, he said, "Does my help

"My friends"

come from the hills?" He says, "No, my help comes from God."

There was a time when we looked to the Atlantic Ocean to protect America in time of war. We looked to the Pacific Ocean that separated us from the Orient. But you can't expect much protection from the Atlantic or the Pacific Ocean now.

We are learning more and more that there doesn't seem to be much human protection. You just can't depend on the help of man these days. In other words, if a man has more sense than you have and is more ingenious as an inventor than you are, he can lick you in battle. A man that's smarter and more scientific than you are may win a war if one comes in your lifetime. Man can't save us. The psalmist cried out, "Vain is the help of man" (Psalm 108:12). If that was so then, what about today?

Sometimes God helps us through a man, but all help comes from God. I've learned over these many years of experience that if I'm going God's way, and there's a gate that needs to be opened, and I don't know how to open the gate, God will have somebody there to open it for me. It will be God's man sent to help me.

When I founded Bob Jones University, the educators said, "You must standardize." And I said, "All right, there's nothing wrong in standardizing. I believe in standardizing." We had to beat the educators at their own game. We had to beat them with standards, so instead of requiring the usual number of hours for graduation, we

God helps through people

added a few more hours.

If you're going God's way and doing God's work, and have satanic opposition, you have to beat the other fellow. Everything else being equal, a Christian *ought* to do a better job than a sinner. If you are a Christian singer, you ought to sing better than an unsaved singer with the same quality of voice you have. There isn't a prima donna who ever lived who couldn't sing a sweeter note if she knew Jesus Christ. There isn't a great architect who couldn't do a better job if he were a Christian. Christianity doesn't take any of the real values away from you; it *adds* to your values.

So we said, "We must have a better school than the others. We must have higher standards. We must have better music and better speech. We must teach better Greek and better Hebrew and better English. We mustn't compromise with standards."

And somebody else came along and said, "Now listen, you need some money." And I said, "You are absolutely right about that. I don't take issue with you, brother." He said, "You're building a school; it's going to take money. What you ought to do is to go contact Mr. So-and-So." If I had contacted everybody that I was told to contact, I'd have been running all over the face of the earth. And about all some of them would have done would have been to say, "We'll consider it." And they would—the rest of their lives. Some of these men are awfully "considerate."

But I didn't have any time to fool around.

"My friends"

We have a campus here in Greenville, South Carolina, that went up in 13 months. We couldn't fool around. I've always had to operate under pressure. We were in a hurry, and I had to go to "the gettin' place" quickly.

The best "getting-place" I've ever found is up in Heaven. I use Washington when I can, but, brother, we're getting in such a fix now, Washington can't help us. And the state capital can't do much for us. And even the bankers can't do much for us. So, when we needed something, we'd say let's go to "the gettin'-place." We'd call God over the telephone (the telephone of prayer) and tell God what we wanted.

This old-time religion will work if you'll just work it. The trouble is, folks have quit working it. Prayer hasn't lost any of its power to move Heaven. Prayer does business. "Whatsoever ye shall ask in prayer, believing, ye shall receive" (Matthew 21:22). "My God shall supply all your need according to his riches in glory by Christ Jesus" (Philippians 4:19). We have a great God.

We've had students come down to school, and they've said to me, "Dr. Bob, I've got enough money to stay a month. But I've prayed over it, and I believe the Lord sent me here."

I know one girl that went through four years of college and became a missionary, yet she came with only enough money for one month. She went as far as she could on the right road and looked up to Heaven, and somehow or other, God sent her money. Now, He sent it through man, but the help didn't come from man, it came from God

God helps through people

through man. Some man sent her the money, because once in a while, she'd get a check. One time the girls in the dormitory went around and paid up her expenses for her. We have a great many girls and boys who come from families that have means, and some who come from homes that don't have much money. That's the reason we've started the Student Loan Endowment Fund—to help students. But you know, *all* help comes from God. "Vain is the help of man."

If you are leaning on the arm of flesh, you haven't got much support now, because it sure is getting weak in this scientific age. But what a God we have! Wouldn't you rather have a little access to Heaven, and be able to slip a few checks through the banks of the sky and get them cashed by Almighty God? They're pretty "well-to-do" up in Heaven. The streets are paved with gold, the walls are jasper, and the gates are solid pearl. They don't even have to pay street tax, pavement taxes, or anything like that up there. It's a wonderful thing.

We tell our students in Bob Jones University, "Be practical. Use good common sense. Keep your feet on the ground. Don't go off on a tangent," and you'll not find a more practical place on earth. Every class is opened with prayer. All public gatherings are opened with prayer. We never have a social get-together that there isn't a little prayer. It's a wonderful thing to scramble prayer in with education and mix it up with business and put it in the kitchen when you're cooking and scramble it in all your life—

"My friends"

we need more of it in this country. Our help comes from God.

"I'm trusting God," as the old preacher said. Whom are you trusting? To whom are you looking for help? If God doesn't help us, there's no help for us. If we get any help from man, it will be because we got help from God Almighty through men. Let's turn to Him in a new surrender and simple Christian faith, and let Him have His way with us.

"O God our help in ages past, our hope for years to come, our shelter from the stormy blast, and our eternal home," we yield ourselves to Thee and trust Thee. We call on Thee for help because help comes from Thee and vain is the help of man. Help us never to forget this. We pray in the name of the Lord Jesus Christ. Amen.

*"The Christian philosophy
is a philosophy of self-denial and self-control;
the satanic philosophy
is a philosophy of 'do as you please,
live your own life.'"*

There are a good many things I do not know. But I could not have maintained my evangelistic position through the years if I had not known something about the emotional and mental processes of the people with whom I deal. In my lifetime, I've seen the philosophy of this country change. When I was a boy, we were taught self-denial and self-control. When we went to school, the educators said, "Take this subject" (Latin, or mathematics, or some subject of that kind). Maybe we didn't like it, but they said we ought to take something we didn't like. They said it taught us self-control and self-denial. They said the thing that you ought to do, whether you liked it or not, was good for you to do. They said it would put muscles in your will and backbone in your character. It would make somebody out of you.

I believe in that philosophy stronger today than ever before in my life. The juvenile delin-

"My friends"

quency wave that's sweeping this country and the divorce mill that's grinding our homes to powder grew out of the satanic philosophy, not the Christian philosophy. Jesus taught men to do right, even if they had to die for the right. He said, "If any man will come after me, let him deny himself, and take up his cross daily, and follow me. For whosoever will save his life shall lose it: but whosoever will lose his life for my sake, the same shall save it" (Luke 9:23-24). It'll cost you something. It'll be hard, it won't be easy, but it'll be a road that will lead to the right place.

Years ago, a great many people accepted the Christian philosophy of self-denial and self-control who would not have accepted the theology I accept as an orthodox, conservative minister of the Gospel. Some people didn't believe in the cleansing blood of Jesus and regenerating grace in the human heart or the necessity of the new birth, but they believed in the Christian philosophy as necessary to build character. We got away from that, and we began to introduce another philosophy in this country. We said, "It's your life, you've got a right to live it. If you want something, you've got a right to have it."

Now, we got that philosophy from the story of Eden—the fall of man. The Devil said to Eve (Genesis 3:1), "Hath God said?" He made her question authority. "Anybody's got a right to tell you that? Oh, has God really said that? Is it so?"

And then she said, "God hath said, Ye shall not eat of it, neither shall ye touch it, lest ye die"

Self-denial and self-control

(Genesis 3:3).

And then he said, "Ye shall not surely die: For God doth know that in the day ye eat thereof, then your eyes shall be opened, and ye shall be as gods, knowing good and evil" (Genesis 3:4-5). "It would be all right, wouldn't it? Why don't you eat it? You've got a right to have what you want."

And Eve heard that philosophy, she ate the fruit, and the next thing she did, she plucked a rose, and there was a thorn on it. There have been thorns on roses from that day till this. That philosophy destroys: it wrecked Paradise, it wrecks human life, and it wrecks civilization.

One of the darkest moments in the Old Testament was when "every man did that which was right in his own eyes" (Judges 17:6). Now we've built that kind of a situation in this nation. That's what's the matter with young people.

When I was a boy, if a fellow married, he married for keeps. He stood there and said, "Until death do us part." And after that if he wasn't exactly happy, he adjusted himself. And they got along pretty well, after all. They were far happier than the people who marry half a dozen times.

One morning a man of the old school of thought had a little fuss with his wife. On his way to work he met a woman and she smiled at him and he said, "Good morning."

And she said, "Good morning."

He said, "You going this way?"

She said, "Yes."

"Where do you work?"

"My friends"

"Well, I work at so and so."

And he said to himself, "She looks good. I imagine she'd be good to a man. She smiles so sweetly. But I'm married. I've got a wife. She was mean to me this morning—we had a little fuss. But I said I was going to keep her until death do us part."

And all day long he's worried, feels guilty, and thinks of that woman who smiled at him. He gets home that night and his wife's all dressed up and she's fixed him a nice supper. He goes in and picks up his paper.

She says, "Did you have a good day?"

"Oh," he says, "very good."

"Well, are you tired?"

"Oh, not much."

He sits there—he feels mean, you know.

And after awhile she says, "Supper's ready."

He goes in the dining room and sits down at the table. She has fixed just exactly what he likes—just exactly. He feels guilty now, for sure.

He says, "Honey, I'm sorry about the way I acted this morning."

She says, "I'm to blame."

He says, "No, I'm to blame."

She says, "No, I'm to blame."

See what held them together? That old-time Christian philosophy of "Do what you ought to do, not what you want to do." This philosophy is necessary to hold families together.

The Devil's philosophy says, "Live your own life. You see that woman; you want her; she wants you. You've got a right to have what you

Self-denial and self-control

want—take her. Break up a home; live as you please."

Now listen, men and women. The Christian philosophy will not take people to Heaven. Christian philosophy will not keep people out of Hell. But it will hold families together; it will hold civilization together; it will keep young people out of the penitentiary. The Christian philosophy helps people live decently in this world. And we need a decent life. Children are growing up by the Devil's philosophy. They're not taught discipline, and they're not taught self-control.

Now, in Bob Jones University, we insist on the Christian philosophy. We say to our young people, "Live a life of self-control. Take some courses you like—take your music, take your speech—but pick out some subject you don't like, and take it. You need something you don't like. Do something you ought to do because it's right to do it whether you like it or not. A man who just does what he wants to do is living on an animal plane. But a man who gets on the plane where man is supposed to live, he does what is right whether he feels like it or not. Do right because it's right to do right!"

Many of us, not even realizing what we are doing, have substituted the satanic philosophy for the Christian philosophy. And we need to get back to that old-time, decent, Christian philosophy of life. We need to learn how to live. Jesus Christ didn't teach folks how to make a living; He taught them how to live. Under ordinary conditions, a man who knows how to live can make a

"My friends"

living. David said, "I have been young, and now am old; yet have I not seen the righteous forsaken, nor his seed begging bread" (Psalm 37:25). He didn't say it didn't exist, but he said he never had seen it.

Now, what we need in this country is a strong emphasis upon old-time, decent Christian philosophy. If we don't get back there, we are ruined. We tell our students in Bob Jones University, and we preach it in the pulpits and on the platforms of this country, "You can do what you ought to do. God doesn't tell you what to do without giving you grace to do it." When God gives you a command, He puts omnipotence back of the command.

Why not begin to make a record. Why don't you stand up and say, "From now on, I'm going to do what I ought to do. If I feel I ought to do a certain thing after getting all the evidence in and checking it, being sensible about it, I'm going to do it; I'm going to do the right thing, feeling or no feeling. I'm going to accept the Christian philosophy."

Of course, if you're not a Christian, I wish you'd accept Christ as your Saviour. You can trust Him as your Saviour. You're not saved by doing good, you're not saved by even being decent. You can be sober and decent and straight and a pretty nice sort of fellow if you have the Christian philosophy of life, but that won't save you. You ought to trust Jesus Christ.

And then, even if you trust Him as your Saviour, you might go out and fail to live the

Self-denial and self-control

Christian philosophy. You might fail to live a life of self-control and self-restraint. You are saved by trusting Christ. You represent Him properly when you live the kind of life you ought to live. He can give you the power to do what you ought to do. Trust Him to do it, and let's put up some standards again.

Our Father, hear us as we pray now for those who read this, that they may be what they ought to be and do what they ought to do. And that we all may live like we ought to live in this world, where there's so much chaos and lawlessness and moral looseness. Hear us, we pray in the name of the Lord Jesus Christ. Amen.

*"The most important light in your
home is not the chandelier in the parlor.
It's that little back hall light."*

My friends, today in the Christian program, we're facing a rather serious peril. It's the peril of what we might call bigness, glamour, limelight—headlines. Everybody seems to have gone crazy about headlines—bigness. Now it's wonderful when, by merit, a man makes the headlines. But all this built-up careerism, this promotion that sells a fellow to the public, is another matter.

We get it in the field of religion; it's very marked sometimes.

I remember once, a few years ago, I said to a preacher friend, who is an editor of a religious paper, "Doctor, there seems to be something wrong with preachers. When I was a boy out in the country of southeast Alabama, we had some of the greatest preachers I have ever known. They were preachers—not great executives. They were not educated very well, but they were great preachers. Almost every town had a great

"My friends"

preacher—some man who had a reputation, a name. They majored in preaching." I said, "What's happened to the country? Now you have a great many very lovely men in the ministry, but you can count on the fingers of your hands the preachers that stand out in America, and most of those men couldn't have made the headlines in the old days." I said, "What's the matter, Doctor?"

"Well," he said, "Dr. Bob, I'll tell you what's the matter. It's careerism."

"What do you mean by that, Doctor? I wonder if you mean what I'm thinking."

"Yes, I mean what I say, careerism. For instance, you go out to Hollywood. There's a starlet out there, a nice attractive girl with average talent; and somebody says to her, 'If you can stand in with the powers that be, you can go to the top.' And she begins to try to get to the top. She has to have contacts to make the top, see. Now, it's the same thing in the ministry, only it's a little more refined. Somebody says to a young preacher when he's taking his seminary course, 'If you want to make a preacher who can get a good job, you better stand in with the powers that be. You take the training in your denominational school and go to your own seminary and get your own denominational stamp on you. And if you do, you'll get a good job, you'll get a good church, you'll stand out.' "

I'm not saying the men who say that are not sincere, but they are putting in the way of young men the most subtle temptation that can be given

Small lights are important

to a young preacher. I fought that battle out when I was a young man. Back in those days, I came to where the road parted. They told me the same thing they tell these young men today; and that's the wrong thing to tell a young preacher. If they'd say to him, "You can be a better preacher; you can win more souls to Jesus Christ; you can do more good," that would be different. That isn't careerism. That's an entirely different thing.

So, without realizing it, most of us have fallen into the idea that if we don't make the headlines, we are no good. But wait just a minute. The biggest things in this world depend upon the least things, things that you never notice, things that never make the headlines.

I was over in Damascus a few years ago and went around the wall of the old city, and the guide said to me, "Right along here is where they let Paul over the wall."

And I stood there and said to myself, "I wonder who they were." Maybe a good Christian woman said to her husband, "Let's get Paul out so they can't kill him. He's a good man. I have a basket here and you get the rope, and we'll just let him down over the wall." We don't even know the names of the people who let him down over the wall, but they were good people. Usually good people stand by good people, and if a man doesn't back God's man, he's usually not a good man himself.

So they let Paul down over the wall. And I stood there and said, "When I get to Heaven, I'm going to ask Paul to introduce me to those

"My friends"

people." They may have been lowly, but I imagine when they let Paul over the wall they brought out "Extras" up in Heaven. I imagine angels ran down the streets saying, "Extra, extra, extra, read all about it, read all about it! Paul's escaped! He's going to preach some more. They tried to kill him. And So-and-So, the saints of God, let him down over the wall."

You can make headlines in Heaven and never make them down here, and some folks who make them down here never make them up in Heaven. We tell our preacher boys, especially, and, of course, we tell all of our students in Bob Jones University, it isn't making headlines down here, it's making headlines in eternity that counts. We've gone crazy on glamour.

When I was a boy, we had a special lamp for company—a kerosene oil lamp. I used to clean the chimney, fill the lamp. Nice people were coming, and we had the nice light fixed up for company. And then we had some little lamps we went around looking for things with. Those little lights. Oh, thank God for little lights. You go down the hall at night on your way to the bathroom, you look up and there's a little light up there shining, not a very bright light, not very attractive. Nobody ever notices it, but it's right up there in the hall. You're walking down there and you look up at it and say, "Thank you, little light, thank you for shining. The glamorous light's not on in the parlor. It's all dark in there. It just shines for company. You shine for protection."

Small lights are important

The older I get, men and women, the more appreciation I have for God's real people—the unnoticed and the unknown—those about whom we never sing and nobody ever says much: a faithful mother who trusts God, lives a Christian life, teaches her baby to pray, brings him up in a Christian home. Thank God for mothers like that. They don't make the headlines. They don't get divorces, you know, and they're not in Hollywood, or on the screen. Their picture never even gets in the paper, but they keep on keeping on, doing right, faithful, living in obscurity. Their children love them. And God never forgets them—the lowly, sweet, good people of the world—the folks who shine where light's needed, and do not shine for the sake of glamour, but shine for the glory of God. Blessed are folks like that.

Now sometimes you people may get discouraged—grinding routine, day in and day out, darning the clothes and the socks, washing the little dirty clothes, and cooking something for folks to eat. But, listen just a minute. Life's not divided into the secular and the sacred—everything's sacred. If you're working for God and trusting God, and living for God, any job you have is a God-given job. "The steps of a good man are ordered by the Lord" (Psalm 37:23). "Commit thy way unto the Lord; trust also in him; and he shall bring it to pass" (Psalm 37:5). And if you are right with God, surrendered to God, you're where God put you, and where God puts you is a wonderful place to be.

You know, it's just as big a thing to be a

"My friends"

mother, if God called you to be a mother, and rear some children, as it is to be a missionary. There's just as much greatness about plowing in the field, if God called you to be a farmer, as there is to stand up and preach, or be an evangelist and make the headlines. I'd like to emphasize that. We've gone crazy in this country on bigness and glamour. I run into so many people who say they had a great crowd, a big this, a big that ... big ... BIG.

Say, thank God for the little things, the unnoticed things and little people who are big in God's sight. For our Lord said, "Whosoever will be great among you, let him be your minister; And whosoever will be chief among you, let him be your servant" (Matthew 20:26-27). If you want to be somebody, don't try to be somebody. Try to serve somebody, and in trying to serve somebody, you become somebody. What a privilege; what an opportunity!

We need to get back to those fundamental principles. A little family altar may be as big in the sight of God as a thousand people praying on a hilltop. One man faithful to God in the closet of prayer may make headlines in Heaven, when a preacher praying to ten thousand people only makes the headlines down here. So remember, the big light, the important light is not the chandelier in the parlor; it's the little back hall light that you never think about, but God never forgets.

Our Father, we lift our hearts to Thee in praise and thanksgiving. We thank Thee for our mother,

Small lights are important

faithful to God in a simple home. For all the good mothers, and good fathers, and faithful, humble saints of God who never went out for glamour, but went out to do the will of God and to seek the glory of God—bless these people today, the average people who are faithful to Jesus Christ. We pray in His name. Amen.

*"A man without enemies
is a man who has accomplished nothing.
You cannot move without producing friction."*

My friends, Bob Jones University at Greenville, South Carolina, is a most remarkable institution. It draws its students from all over the world, gives all the fine arts without additional cost above academic tuition, and stands without apology for the old-time religion and the absolute authority of the Bible. It doesn't compromise.

I'm not really an educator; I'm a preacher and an evangelist. I stay in character when I'm on the platform and when I'm in the pulpit and when I'm talking over the radio. I don't like to hear a preacher get out of character. I was at a business club one time, and a certain preacher was introduced. And this famous preacher stood up and told some very questionable jokes. I was sitting by the side of a man of the world who wasn't a Christian. This man said, "You know, I haven't any respect for him. He ought to stay in character."

"My friends"

The statement, "A man without enemies is a man who has no accomplishment; you cannot move without producing friction," applies not only to the ministry, it applies to all walks of life. It holds everywhere. Even a man in the underworld who has no enemies is a man who has done nothing. The underworld has its standards, wicked as they are. And a man who succeeds in the underworld, (if there's such a thing as succeeding in the underworld—of course, there isn't any true success there), succeeds by moving and producing friction.

That statement also holds in the educational world. There are all sorts of schools in America. Many religious schools are having a hard time getting along. Many of them are struggling for existence. They may have a convention or conference, or state, or even a whole denomination back of them. We started a school called Bob Jones University, and people wonder how we get along with no conference, no convention, and no assembly back of us. They go by our buildings and look at the modern architecture. They see the happy students from all over the world. They find our institution without the problems that others have. We don't have any trouble. Everybody is loyal—the faculty is loyal, the students are loyal. We have no jealousies or strife. We have high standards of culture. We have strict discipline as the world calls discipline. People criticize you and say, "You can't do those things in this day and time." That used to worry me, but it doesn't worry me any more. It doesn't bother

Action produces friction

me now because I know human nature. I didn't as a young man. When I was a young man, I said, "If you love everybody, and you're sweet to everybody, everybody will love you." But I learned from bitter experience that that isn't true.

So, you can't move without producing friction. That holds in every walk of life. People can't forgive you if you pass them on the road and they have to "take your dust." Did you ever drive down a road that wasn't paved and your old car was all rattling? A fellow in a nice new car went by you, and you had to "take his dust"? You have to have some good old-time religion to smile and say, "Nice car, isn't it? Wish mine would run like that." It takes grace, doesn't it? Sam Jones (no relative of mine, but a unique old-time evangelist) was probably the greatest preacher who ever stood on an evangelistic platform in America. When he was at his best, Sam Jones used to say, "Sure does take a lot of grace to say 'Amen' when a fellow is doing something you'd like to do and can't do." And that's true in life. Don't worry about your enemies. If achievement made you have enemies, it's a compliment to you. You ought to be proud that at least people know you're in the country.

You never hear people coming around and kicking a dead man. Billy Sunday was one of the closest, sweetest friends I ever had. And I remember when Billy Sunday died. Nobody cussed him. I read some newspapers, and how well they spoke of him, after he was dead, and his deaf ears couldn't hear.

"My friends"

And I remember when William Jennings Bryan was being cussed by nearly everybody. There never was a nobler, finer, sweeter, more upright man than William Jennings Bryan. He was one of the greatest and purest Christian men I've ever known. I was in the New York convention when Mr. Bryan was trying to keep his hand on the throttle and keep that thing straight. I sat through that convention 12 days in the gallery as an observer. Talk about studying psychology and folks being crazy! Don't talk to me about *religious* fanatics! You go to a Democratic convention or a Republican convention where judges and governors and United States senators march up and down and yell and carry flags and banners. I never saw a religious campaign in my life as crazy as a political convention. Nobody thinks anything about that—they're crazy about politics. Well, I sat in that convention and studied it and Mr. Bryan. It was the last convention he ever attended. And I never shall forget when he said in his speech, "This may be the last one I'll ever attend." The people just booed him, but he didn't flinch. Then when he died, you ought to have read the papers. I knew some of these papers that used to pick on him and say mean things about him. But when he was dead, I saw a cartoon in one of them with Bryan sitting there in his office, and "WJB" on the door. The angel of death came and knocked on the door and said, "The chief witness, the chief witness called." When he was dead, everybody was kind to him.

Action produces friction

You don't hear anybody saying anything against Jesus now. At least no decent person says anything against Jesus anymore. A great many people don't accept Him as their Saviour. A great many of them reject Him as Lord, but they throw kisses at His goodness. But my, what they said about Christ when He was here. He went to the cross with men mocking and spitting at Him. As Christ moved to Calvary, He produced friction.

You can't move without producing friction. You can't stand for Jesus Christ without producing friction. "Woe unto you," the Bible says, "when all men shall speak well of you!" (Luke 6:26). *Woe* be unto you. If you live godly, He says you will suffer persecution. It has always cost something to be a Christian. The Christian moves with God, and God moves across the current of the age, not with the age. The current of the age is the current of the flesh and looseness and selfishness, and God runs across that current. If you walk with God, the current's against you. But if you have God, it doesn't matter who's against you. "If God be for us, who can be against us?" (Romans 8:31). They *can* be against you, but it doesn't matter if they *are* against you if you have Christ for you.

Thank God for the enemies that you have if you have made them right. But one word of warning: you ought not to deliberately choose to make them. You ought to live right, and faithful, and be a Christian and loyal to Jesus Christ, but do the good works that you do the best you can and don't let what folks say against you be true.

"My friends"

It's all right for them to say bad things against you, as long as they are not true.

Our Father, help us to be true to Jesus Christ, true to our convictions, faithful to the end, we pray in His ever-precious name. Amen.

"A man whose supreme desire is to do what is right has no difficulty finding out what is right."

My friends, I am not a literary genius or a great scholar, but early in life I learned a few fundamental principles about life. I learned that a man who doesn't know what to do, if he wants to do right, can go ask somebody. In other words, he can borrow brains.

When I got ready to build a school, I said certain fundamental principles are the same whether you are running a store, a university, a peanut stand, or a government. Now, the application of those principles may change. How you work them out in the educational field may be a little different from the way you work them out in business or the way you work them out in the field of religion. You may apply them in a little different way according to the circumstances under which you operate, but they never change. So, while I don't know much about this education business and don't claim to know, my son, who is

"My friends"

the president of the school, knows, and the other people associated with him know. They're all authorities in their field. But, of course, I learned a good many things before they got into books. You know, you can get knowledge out of books, and you can get it out of the minds and hearts of people.

When I was a young preacher just starting as a country boy, I didn't know much about the Bible, either. It's remarkable how a fellow can get along. You can take John 3:16 and get converted and then take John 3:16, "For God so loved the world, that he gave his only begotten Son, that whosoever believeth in him should not perish, but have everlasting life" and just go around and tell people that and get them converted. So, I was having a great many conversions before I knew much about the Bible. But if people would ask me something, I'd always say, "I don't know," if I didn't know. I never claimed to know. People try to help you if you don't talk too wise. If you talk so wise, they'll let you go on your own way and make a mess of things. So, if they asked me what a Bible verse meant, I'd always say, "Well, I don't know." I was just a boy fifteen years old. They'd ask me if we'd know each other in Heaven, and all I'd say to them was, "Well, I don't know why you wouldn't. I don't know—I haven't been to Heaven yet. Looks to me like we'd know each other in Heaven, we've got that much sense down here. I think I'll have as much in Heaven as I have here, but of course, I haven't been up there. I can't say

Desire to do right

positively about that."

But I soon learned something in dealing with people. And then I saw what I had learned in the Bible. I never had a fellow come to me in my life who was really sincere and wanted to do right but what he could find out what to do, if that's what he wanted. And so one day I opened my Bible and read where Jesus said, "If any man will do his will, he shall know of the doctrine" (John 7:17). In other words, Jesus said, "If you want to do right, you won't have any trouble knowing." It isn't so hard to know as it is to want to know. A great many people say they want to know and don't mean it.

One time a boy at Bob Jones University came to my office and sat down to talk to me. This boy wanted to get married right away. He didn't have any money, he was too young, his girl was too young, and he wasn't through school. He asked me if I thought it would be all right for him to get married. I asked him a good many questions. Then I said, "Well, I'd wait. I'd get my education finished. You have one more year here. It'll go by very quickly." Of course, I had a hard time making him believe that, as desperately in love as he was. And I gave him advice and thought everything was over. And then he started in to argue with me and convince me that I ought to say it would be all right. Oh, he made a wonderful speech. He'd worked out all the arguments. I said, "Now wait a minute. Did you come to get me to tell you to do what you want to do?"

"My friends"

You know, most people that come around for advice want you to encourage them to do what they are inclined to do. I learned that when I was just a boy preacher. Somebody comes to me and tells me this and that and the other and says, "Now, what do you think about so and so?" And I'd tell them, "Well, so and so," and they'd go to arguing with me and trying to convince me that I'm wrong after they've asked me what to do. They want to do right, but they want to do what *they* want to do.

Now, that's in line with the Bible. The Bible says, "A doubleminded man is unstable in all his ways" (James 1:8). Did you ever see a drunk man go down the road? He's had a lot of whiskey, and he wants to walk straight. He tries to straighten up, throw his shoulders back and hold up his head. And he starts down a step or two straight and he goes to stagger from one side to the other. Now, he has a little consciousness down in his mind that a fellow ought not to be drunk in public, and he ought to hold up his shoulders and walk straight, kinda wants to do it, you know, but that whiskey pulls him around from one side to the other. That's the way it is with men in this world. They start out and say, "I want to do the right thing." Then ambition calls, and ambition pulls them over to the other side of the road. And then they say, "This isn't right," and they get back on the other side, and they just keep wobbling from one side to the other. Haven't you seen folks like that? You've got some neighbors like that. You may be like that yourself.

Desire to do right

Now, if you want to know what's right, it's the easiest thing in the world. The trouble is you would like to do right, but you also want to do what you want to do, whether it's right or not. So you just stay in a mess all the time.

I made up my mind long ago as a young Christian that when I came to an issue in life, I'd just sit down and face the issue, and say, "I'm going to try to find out what's right, and I'm going to do that." I met that issue one time in Bob Jones College before my son became president. We had a girl in school and this girl was a very attractive kind of girl, but she wasn't any good as a student, and she wasn't exactly right, either. She wasn't our kind. But her daddy was a pretty nice sort of fellow; he had a lot of money, too, and the school was up against it in those days—we needed money. One day we had to expel that girl. Of course, we have a discipline committee made up of students and faculty. But folks always blamed me if somebody was expelled. I felt bad about it, to tell you the truth, because her daddy was going to give us $100,000 and I needed $100,000. We had an awful struggle in those days. So, the girl came in and she asked me to talk to the committee. I said, "I can't do it. They did right. You'll have to go home. Your father's a friend of mine, and I'm sorry to see this happen, but I can't let friendship affect me in a matter like this. You'll have to go home. We're going to run a Christian school and you're not in line here. You're doing the institution harm by not holding up our standards, and you won't be the right

"My friends"

representative of this school when you go out. So you'll have to go." And you ought to have seen the letter that girl's daddy wrote me. Brother, you know, he set that paper on fire. He said, in so many words, "I'd let everybody on that campus starve before I'd send you any money." Well, I expected that. But you have to do right, don't you?

You know, if you *want* to do right, you don't have any trouble knowing what's right. It's easy. All you've got to do is to ask God, and if God's already told you, you don't have to go back and ask Him. If it's contrary to the Ten Commandments, it's wrong. If it's contrary to the Sermon on the Mount, it's wrong. If it's contrary to the Gospel of Jesus Christ, it's wrong.

But it's hard to *do* right. Sometimes it's awfully hard. It takes faith, and character, and manhood, and womanhood—you know it isn't easy to stand. A soldier on a battlefield has no harder time to stand than some of you in the quiet, ordinary, routine battles of life. It's not easy for a preacher, not easy for a schoolteacher, not easy for anybody. But do right. Those two little words are such big little words, and you can know what's right if you want to know. And if you know what's right, God can give you grace to *do* what's right.

Our Father, we look to Thee today for help and strength. We need Thee. We are weak, all of us. We need strength that comes from God. But if God gives us strength, we can meet any issue and do right. Help every one of us to make up our minds

Desire to do right

that we are going to do right from now on, regardless of the cost. Keep us by Thy power faithful to Thee, for Jesus' sake. Amen.

"There is no tragedy as tragic as combining high mentality with low morality."

My friends, in this day a good deal of emphasis is put on what we call "intellectuality." We talk about a man's I.Q. We try to find out not so much what the man knows, but what he *could* know—his capacity for knowledge. But knowledge never has saved anybody. The Bible says, "If the Son therefore shall make you free, ye shall be free indeed" (John 8:36). But knowledge doesn't save men.

Your capacity for knowledge doesn't mean that you have a natural capacity for goodness. You may be well trained as far as this world is concerned and be very immoral. Hitler had a pretty good mind. He was a genius. You can't deny the fact that he was a brilliant man—he was a dynamic personality. You cannot deny the fact that Napoleon Bonaparte and Alexander the Great had brains. We read of great historical characters who had good I.Q.'s who committed

"My friends"

crimes. And I have known some people that didn't have a very high I.Q. that were pretty good people.

I think a fellow that knows how to trust God, though he may not measure very high as far as I.Q. is concerned, is a pretty smart man. We had a speaker on our platform some time ago at Bob Jones University, a very prominent statesman and a very charming Christian man. He was talking about Christianity in business, politics, and government. He said one of the most significant things I've ever heard. And he was right about it, if you stop to think. I'm not trying to quote his exact words, but here's what he said in substance, "I don't like the idea of trusting my business affairs to a man in office who hasn't got enough business sense to make preparation for eternity." Now, the older I get, the more I realize that speaker was right. We read about that man in the Bible who had such a great harvest he had to build new barns to hold it and then walked out and sat down on his porch and figuratively speaking folded his hands and said, "I've got plenty. My barns are full. I've got enough laid up for many years. I'll eat and drink and take life easy" (Luke 12:18-19). And Jesus Christ said, "He is a fool." He had enough sense to run a farm, enough sense to make a crop, enough sense to save what he made, enough sense to build a new barn—he had enough sense for all that. But was he smart?

A man isn't necessarily smart because he sings well, or plays an instrument well, or paints

Mixing high mentality with low morality

a wonderful picture. He may have a flash of genius that will make him do that. Genius is not always brains; it has brains mixed up with it, but isn't always brains. Are these people smart?

Once in a while, you see a man that has a high I.Q., but he has low morality. That's a tragedy. He should know better. He ought to have been somebody, but he played the fool. The prodigal son, after he wandered away from the father's house and his father's table, began to think it over. He said, "How many hired servants of my father's have bread enough and to spare, and I perish with hunger! I will arise and go to my father, and will say unto him, Father,... make me as one of thy hired servants" (Luke 15:17-19). In other words, he said, "You know, I am a fool. I could have been somebody, and I'm sitting over here feeding hogs in a faraway country and haven't anything left. The servants in my father's house are better off than I am, and I'm a son." He said, "I'm going to get up and go back home, and I'm not going to ask for any recognition except a servant's place. I'm not going to ask to be a son. I'm going to ask him to make me the hired servant and let me work around the house." He had enough sense to get out of trouble and to know what to do. But a fellow who gets up against it and goes out and blows a hole in his head or jumps in the river or gets in a boat and jumps out is a fool. The intelligent fellow that gets up against it says, "How can I get this thing fixed? I can't be what I could have been, but I'll be the best I can."

"My friends"

The prodigal son never was the same after that. Don't make him a hero. The hero was the father that took him back. I'm tired of seeing people make that boy a hero. No man's a hero that makes the mess he made. That prodigal son was never the same again. But when you know you're in a mess, you ought to have enough sense to know how to get out of it. You ought to have enough sense to know what to do. You respect the prodigal son for that. He made the best of the situation.

Somebody today who had a good mother and good father, and maybe had educational advantages and opportunities and the proper teaching, and had pretty good intelligence has played the fool's game and made a mess of your life. You've got things in such a terrible jam and here you are and you don't know what to do. I'll tell you what to do: look up to Jesus Christ. All my life I've had people come to me in my evangelistic campaigns with tragic stories. People that killed their own babies, folks that murdered their own mothers, men that killed their wives. All my life I've heard them in evangelistic work. You know, we old-time evangelists preached people under conviction. We'd run a campaign a week or ten days before we'd ask anybody to come forward in the meeting. Sinners would get so convicted, they couldn't sleep at night. And I've had them to keep me awake at night, knocking at my door at the hotel to beg me to tell them what to do. They told their story of awful sins they'd committed. And I sat down with them, and told

Mixing high mentality with low morality

them what to do, how they could make the best of their situations, and told them, "You may not be all you could've been, but from now on you can be all you ought to be."

If I were a sinner, living like some of you are living, I'd have enough practical common sense to get right with God. Some of you are on your way to doom. Some of you folks are going to be in the worst jam you ever imagined. You can't conceive of what's ahead of you. Don't go on in sin; you can't beat the game. Why don't you turn to Jesus Christ and trust Him as your Saviour and come clean with Him? Start on a clean sheet and write a clean record. Be everything you can be from now on by the grace of God.

Our Father, help them to do it. Speak to them today. Spirit of God, brood over them. Help them to surrender to You and to trust You and turn to You for saving mercy, we pray in the name of the Lord Jesus. Amen.

> *"It is never right to do something wrong, even to get an opportunity to do something that is right."*

My friends, I'd like to tell you a little story of an experience I had some time ago with a preacher of the Gospel. This gentleman is a nice man, and I like him personally. But he's absolutely wrong in his philosophy.

He is a religious conservative who believes the Bible from cover to cover. He believes that the Bible *is* the Word of God, not that it just *contains* the Word of God. He believes that Jesus Christ is the virgin-born Son of God, that when He was in this world He was God manifested in the flesh. He believes that when Jesus Christ went to the cross, He bore our sins in His body, and He died a substitutionary and vicarious death at Calvary. He believes that Jesus Christ was buried and the third day He rose again from the dead. He believes that the Lord Jesus Christ went to Heaven, that He's up there at the Father's right hand, interceding for His people. And he believes

"My friends"

that Jesus Christ is the only hope of a lost sinner, and that He is what He said He was, "the way, the truth, and the life" (John 14:6).

I believe that, too. I do not believe that Jesus Christ is *a* way to God. I believe He's the *only* way to God, and that there is salvation in no other name except the name of the Lord Jesus Christ.

Now, the statement I've made concerning what this preacher believes and what I personally accept contains all the essential fundamentals of the Christian faith. Bob Jones University, which I founded, is built upon these essential, fundamental truths accepted by all conservative Christians.

Now, I said to my preacher friend, "Your philosophy is wrong. You are supporting an educational program that is not in line with your Christian position: a program that is not in line with your spiritual understanding, even on the mission field."

"Well," he said, "I know, Bob, that's true. I don't agree with them, you know. And my church is a pretty sound church. We believe the fundamentals. But," he said, "here's what I do. By going ahead and supporting that program, I get an opportunity to preach the Gospel. I can't deny myself this opportunity. I have to preach the Gospel, you know. I'm called to preach. And if I go ahead and support the program, I'll have a church and get a chance to preach, and look how much good I can do!"

But I said, "Wait a minute. Who ever told you, my friend, that it's right to do something wrong

It is never right to do wrong

to get a chance to do right? It's not right to disobey God, even to get an opportunity to obey God. Jesus said, 'Go ye into all the world, and preach the gospel to every creature' (Mark 16:15). But He didn't say, 'Now, compromise to do it.' And, my friend, you don't have to compromise. The Bible says clearly that if a man comes along bringing any other doctrine contrary to the essential doctrines of the Christian faith, or the doctrines of Christ, if we bid that man Godspeed, we are a party to what that man is doing." And I said to my friend, "You're not only bidding him Godspeed, you're buying him a ticket to go to the mission field to disseminate false doctrines. You're also helping pay his salary in the school where he teaches, though he's a modernistic scholar teaching everything contrary to what you preach and believe. Now that's wrong. There's no way to make that right."

God Almighty is not the author of compromise and never has been. It's wrong to do wrong, and compromise is doing wrong. If you believe that Jesus Christ is the virgin-born Son of God, you have no moral right to support a movement that says that Jesus Christ was conceived out of wedlock and was an illegitimate child. If Jesus Christ died on the cross to save sinners, and if without the shedding of His blood there is no remission for sin, then you have no right to support a movement that repudiates this fundamental truth of the Christian faith. If Jesus Christ literally rose from the dead and you deny this truth, according to the Bible you have no hope. Paul would say, "Why go ahead with the business? If Christ is still dead we have no basis for our faith." "If Christ be not risen, then is our preaching vain, and your faith is also vain" (I Corinthians 15:14).

Now, I'm an American citizen. I believe in separation of church and state. I think if I go into a high school to speak, I ought to be a gentleman. Under our system of government, I ought not go into a high school and force upon people, who don't agree with me, certain positions that I may accept. For instance, I'd never go into a high school and offend anybody. I go there as a guest, as an American, to go as far as I can on the right road. And I've said so many times, compromise is not going as far as you can on the right road. Compromise is going any distance on the wrong road. It's compromise for me to stand up in my own pulpit or on a platform where I'm conducting an evangelistic campaign and support something that's wrong while I preach something that's right. It's another thing for me to speak at a Rotary Club or a Kiwanis Club, or in a public school, or some university, and go as far as I can on the right road.

When I was in Japan some time ago, I spoke to the Imperial University; I spoke in a Buddhist school; I didn't compromise anything. I didn't go as far in the Buddhist school as I'd go on the platform at Bob Jones University, but I didn't sell out Jesus Christ. I went as far as I could under the circumstances. It's another thing to double-cross Jesus Christ.

It is never right to do wrong

And Jesus Christ is being double-crossed in this country in Christian pulpits, on platforms that are supposed to be Christian, and in denominations that have a good, sound, fundamental creed.

I have the utmost respect for a Jew who is faithful to his Judaism and honest and straight. I have the utmost respect for a Roman Catholic who stands for what he believes. I have the profoundest respect for every evangelical, orthodox, Protestant preacher in the world who preaches what he believes and won't compromise what he believes.

I have the utmost contempt for any man on earth who claims to be an orthodox man who will compromise with things contrary to his orthodoxy in order to please somebody, or in order to stand up and say, "Well, I have a chance to preach by doing this." You've no right to do wrong to get a chance to do right.

And I want to testify to this: never one time in my life have I compromised my ministry. I've tried to be a gentleman, but I haven't compromised, and I'm not going to compromise. I believe the Bible from cover to cover; I believe Jesus is the Son of God and died on the cross to save sinners and rose again from the dead and is the only hope for a lost world.

Bob Jones University believes that. We don't apologize to anybody anywhere in the world for it. We are not going to do wrong, even to get a chance to do something that is right.

Our Heavenly Father, we are living in a day of

"My friends"

compromise, in a day when we are sacrificing principle on the altar of convenience. Give us some good old rugged Christian character in this country that will stand the test of the day in which we are living. And make us all what we ought to be—faithful to Thee, we pray in the name of the Lord Jesus Christ. Amen.

"Heaven and Hell are in opposite directions, and no man can travel both ways at the same time."

I sometimes wonder just how I fit into this very peculiar age in which we are living. When I was a boy, everything was black or white. Now things are a dull gray. When I was a boy, we said, "This is right and that's wrong, and you can't do right doing wrong." And we said, "There are just two ways, a good way and a bad way; a road that leads to Heaven, and a road that leads to Hell." When I was a boy we used to say, "You're either saved or you're lost. There's no middle ground to it." We said, "You can't be neutral; you're one or the other, either a Christian or a sinner. You're going to Heaven or Hell." That's the way I was reared. That was pretty good rearing, too.

I met a man who said to me, "I don't see how anybody could believe in Hell."

I said, "You don't?"

"No, I don't see how you could believe in Hell."

"Well, I've seen 10,000 hells on this earth. I've

"My friends"

seen sin turn a happy home into a hell. Don't tell me there's no hell. Sin produces hell on this earth."

Yes, all the hell in this world was made by man. Sin produced it. The first time sin put its foot down on this earth it destroyed Paradise. "Paradise Lost" is one of the tracks that sin made when it came to this earth. Every graveyard you ever saw is a little footprint that sin made. Sin's a terrible thing. It's awful to do wrong. The Bible says, "The wages of sin is death" (Romans 6:23). Don't treat sin lightly.

According to the conservative religious position which I accept, and for which Bob Jones University stands, and which all orthodox evangelical Christians accept, regardless of the denominational affiliation, this is the position: When Jesus Christ was on this earth, He was God manifest in the flesh. And one day, God-manifest-in-the-flesh went up on a hilltop and was nailed to a cross. And He bowed His head and died under the weight of the sin of the world.

If sin nailed Jesus Christ to the cross, sin is terrible enough to send men to Hell. I have no trouble believing in Hell. Don't tell me there's no such thing. There's bound to be some kind of Hell.

There used to live in the South, before my day, a famous old preacher by the name of Muncy. He preached some great sermons. I read two volumes of his sermons when I was a boy, and I've never forgotten them. There were a good many things Muncy said Hell might be. Oh, the picture he painted! He said, "There is a place of future rewards for the righteous; therefore, there's a place of future punishment for the wicked."

It's either Heaven OR Hell

People say they don't believe in being Hell-scared. Well, you'd better be Hell-scared than Hell-scorched. I'm afraid to sin. I think I'm about as game as the average fellow, but I've always been afraid to sin.

You'd better come clean. You can't be going to Heaven and Hell at the same time. Sin's an awful thing. It would be better to go out West and find a nest of rattlesnakes and lie down and sleep with them than to sleep in the arms of sin like some of you are sleeping. You'd better go down to the power house in your town and play with a few thousand volts of electricity than to play with sin like some of you are playing. You'd better reach up into the dark pavilion of a storm cloud and play with forked lightning than to play with sin like some of you young people are playing with sin.

I've seen them play with it. And I've seen them behind prison bars. They've said, "Oh, how did I do it? Why did I get into this mess? How did I get here? How could this thing be happening to me?" There isn't a sin any sinner ever committed that every sinner under proper provocation could not commit. Sin's an awful thing.

Now when God Almighty made man, He made him a free moral agent. If you didn't have a free will, you wouldn't be a man. You have the power to choose between right and wrong, between God and the Devil, between Heaven and Hell. You have the power.

And don't tell me that everybody goes to the same place when they die. Don't tell me that. One time a man was put in an insane asylum, not because anybody had anything against him, but because he was incurable. He was a hopeless,

"My friends"

raving, insane man who was dangerous.

Well, that man in the asylum was a terribly crazy man. He would kill his wife and his children. And they *had* to shut him up. That wasn't cruel; it was kind to put him in an asylum and lock him up in a cell. It was necessary.

Hell is God's hospital for incurables. If you are a poor, miserable, hopeless sinner, God can't allow you into Heaven. You'd destroy it. Remember, when sin entered Paradise, Paradise was destroyed. And the devil was cast out of Heaven—cast out because he was a rebel. God is the governmental head of His universe, and the subjects of this universe must have respect for the authority of Almighty God.

God loves you. He loves you so much, He sent His Son to die for you. Jesus Christ "was wounded for our transgressions, he was bruised for our iniquities" (Isaiah 53:5). And if you're lost, don't blame anybody but yourself. You don't *have* to go to Hell. If you're going to go to Hell, go like a man.

I saw a fellow one time in jail; he looked into my face and said, "I deserve to be here. I broke the law. I didn't have to come; I took a chance and lost, and I'm here. And I'm going to take it like a man."

And if I were a sinner and were going to reject Jesus Christ and die and go to Hell, I'd take it like a man. I'd go down there and say, "Well, I sinned against God. I could have been different; I didn't have to be lost. I could have been in Heaven, but I'm in Hell."

And I want to bring you this message: you're not going to Heaven and Hell, too. You're going to one or the other. You are right or you are

It's either Heaven OR Hell

wrong. You are saved or you are lost. You are on God's side or the Devil's side. You're either saved or you're not saved.

I wouldn't take any chance with my soul, if I were you.

Every year when we open school at Bob Jones University, we ask all the students to face the issue. We say you're either a Christian or you're not a Christian. And if you're not a Christian, you can become a Christian. Jesus Christ is able to save you. And the first night we opened our school, we had 42 young people to accept Christ. The first one of that group, the first convert, is now a Presbyterian minister, the pastor of a strong church in the South. He was a skeptic; we didn't know it when he enrolled. We try not to take people who are not Christians, because our business in this school is to train Christian leaders; that is, we take young people who are Christians and train them to be Christian leaders. But if they do come to us unsaved, we try to get them saved.

And I want to appeal to you now. If you're not saved, why don't you accept Jesus Christ?

Our Father, when we get to Heaven by the grace of God, help us to meet somebody there who read this message and who made the decision. We trust Thee for Thy help and Thy saving grace, and pray to Thee for the salvation of souls. In the name of the Lord Jesus. Amen.

"You do what you ought not to do, because you do not do what you ought to do."

My friends, so many people say, "Quit your meanness and be a Christian." I've heard some people say, "Give up sin, and take Christ." People mean well by that, but that's not the true Bible approach. The Bible approach is a little different. It isn't "Quit your sin and accept Christ," it's "Accept Christ and quit your sin." It isn't "Quit your meanness and become a Christian," it's "Become a Christian and quit your meanness."

The exhortations in the Bible about how to live are exhortations largely to Christian people. For instance, we read, "Let us lay aside every weight, and the sin that doth so easily beset us, and let us run with patience the race that is set before us" (Hebrews 12:1). That's addressed to Christian people who are in a race. They want to win a contest. They're compared to people that go out and win a race to get a corruptible crown. Paul said, "We Christians are in the business of running a race to get an incorruptible crown." "Now they do it to obtain a corruptible crown; but we an incorruptible" (I Corinthians 9:25). He's not talking about going to Heaven; he's talking about a special reward given to Christian people who keep their bodies under.

You don't hear God telling sinners to quit their sins. He doesn't go up and down the country telling the children of the Devil how to live. The Bible says, we "are all the children of God by faith in Christ Jesus" (Galatians 3:26). It's strange how this "universal fatherhood of God" idea got started. There isn't one word in the Bible about it. The Bible says, "As many as received him, to them gave he power to become the sons of God" (John 1:12). We become children of God when we accept Jesus Christ as personal Saviour. God tells His children that they are witnesses, and they are to let their light shine, and they ought to live victorious lives. But God doesn't order the Devil's children around. He tells the Devil's children, "If you'll come on over here, I'll take you and save you and make you one of my children. And then I'll teach you how to live."

We read in the Bible that the Thessalonians turned *to* God from idols—not *from* idols to God. Some of you are going to a certain place and you want to go to another place that's in the opposite direction. You simply turn around and start the other way. The way to get rid of the sin problem is not just to saw a limb off of the tree of sin or give up some little habit. The way to do the thing is to turn to Jesus Christ—that puts

Do what you ought to do

your back to sin. The Thessalonians "turned to God from idols to serve the living and true God" (I Thessalonians 1:9).

Turn "to God from idols"—that's conversion; "serve the living and true God"—that's Christian service; "wait for his Son from Heaven" (I Thessalonians 1:10)—that's Christian hope. If you are not right, you should turn to God from idols. That's the beginning of the thing.

Of course, you're not going to Heaven because you just quit certain things; you can spend your life sawing limbs off of the tree. That's not what's the matter with you. The trouble is with the tree. The Bible says that "a corrupt tree bringeth forth evil fruit" (Matthew 7:17). You don't have to do anything to do wrong, just let the tree bear it's own fruit. If you're a sinner, you will sin. If you're a liar, you will lie. If you're a thief, you will steal if you get a chance. If your heart is unclean, you will do unclean things. If you're selfish, you will love money. All a sinner has to do is to be natural. All the good things that you do as a sinner are more or less unnatural for you. When you become a Christian, you get a supernatural experience. You get something in your heart. You love what you didn't used to love, and hate what you didn't used to hate. And you get something inside of you that drives you down the road of God's purpose and God's way for your life.

Now we Christian people should lay aside the weights and the burdens that beset us. And some of us have faults. If I'm running down this road

"My friends"

with a grindstone under one arm and a jug of whiskey in the other hand, the jug of whiskey is a sin and the grindstone is a weight. I say, "Well, I'm going to get rid of the jug of liquor," so I throw it down, but I still can't run because I've got a grindstone that is too heavy.

A great many Christian people have a lot of faults. They'll say, "That's just my way; people think I'm mad when I'm not mad." If people think you're mad when you're not mad, you ought to change; that's a fault. You shouldn't make people think you're angry when you're not angry. As a Christian, you should get rid of anything that hinders you. It doesn't matter what it is. We Christians have things wrong with us. Sometimes we do things we ought not to do. We shouldn't, but some of us do. We ought to get rid of the thing.

But now, you folks that are not right with God, what you ought to do is to get right. All the things that you've been doing, you've just been doing naturally, that's all. You just went and did them. And if you didn't watch yourself, you'd do lots more mean things than you're doing. So the thing you do that you ought not to do, you do because you don't do what you *ought* to do. Now, you ought to get right with God.

A fellow said to me one time, "Dr. Bob, I was born wrong."

I said, "You can be born again and born right this time. You can get a new birth."

The fellow said, "But I'm just made that way. I've just got the Devil in me."

Do what you ought to do

"I know that. I know you have, but Jesus can cast out the Devil. He can make you over again."

Somebody reading this right now has said a thousand times, "I'm never going to do that again." And you cried about it, and maybe you even told God you wouldn't do it. But you went and did it. You're a slave bound by the chains of slavery and sin. You're all tied up with the Devil. What you ought to do is to get right with Jesus Christ. He can make you right. He can deliver you. He can set you free. He never saw anybody He couldn't set free. He woke up dead people and brought them out of the grave when He was here on earth. And if you're in the grave of sin, bound by the awful chains of the Devil, you can be made free. I've seen Jesus do that thousands of times.

In Bob Jones University we say, "Education won't save you. Education will press your pants and shine your shoes, and comb your hair and dress you up so you can move around among people and make contacts, but you can be fixed up nice and still have a mean heart." Did you know the meanest sinner in your town can dress up as well as the nicest fellow in town? If you dress a sinner up and let him walk down the street, you can't tell whether he's a Christian or a sinner. But he's got a heart in there that's wrong. The Bible says, "The heart is ... desperately wicked" (Jeremiah 17:9). The natural heart literally means, "incurably sick." What you need is a new heart.

Now, in religious services, we say, "Give your heart to God." I know what we mean when we say

"My friends"

give your heart to God, but that's not really Bible language. "Son, give me thy heart" is addressed to Christians, or people who are right with God. God doesn't really want your heart if you're a sinner. He wants to *give* you a new heart.

So if you come to Jesus, He will give you a new heart, and a heart set free from sin. And then you can go out in the world and live right. You'll *want* to live right. You'll have power to live right. And you won't be doing the things you've been doing, if you'll get right with God.

Notice this one verse, "Whosoever is born of God doth not commit sin" (I John 3:9). The underlying Greek idea is this—notice it now: He that is born of God does not *practice* sin. He cannot practice sin because His seed remains within him. That's the Greek idea. In other words, when you get this new nature, you get something in your heart; you just can't go on habitually like you've been going. So the bad things that you've been doing, you've been doing because you didn't have what you ought to have. If you'll do what you ought to do—get right with Jesus Christ—then you'll quit doing what you ought not to do. That's God's method and God's process. You can restrain yourself and go ahead in this world—it's better to be moral than immoral—but that's not enough. You need Jesus Christ, and you can have Him if you want Him. He says, "Look unto me, and be ye saved, all the ends of the earth" (Isaiah 45:22).

Our Father, help somebody who isn't a Christian to come to You to trust You, and help

Do what you ought to do

him to yield himself to Christ. And give victory through Jesus Christ to the defeated Christians who have read this message. We pray in the ever precious name of the Lord Jesus Christ. Amen.

*"No man is high born
until he is born from on high."*

My friends, in my wide contacts and experiences in dealing with people, I've been surprised and often shocked at the conception some people have of what we call "Christian education." People talk about Christian education when they mean religious education.

The Lord Jesus Christ was the greatest teacher the world ever knew. One day quite a scholarly gentleman named Nicodemus went to see the Lord Jesus Christ and said, "I'd like to matriculate in your school. I've been thinking it over, and I've come to the conclusion that no man could do what You're doing unless God were with Him."

This idea is the highest reach of the human intellect in its effort to grasp the spiritual things that have been wrought in this earth. The average man who doesn't know God, but knows human nature and knows the mental processes of man and knows human limitations, may conclude from seeing certain things that those things are

"My friends"

out of the realm of the human. There must be something from another world that produces it.

Nicodemus was an honest, sincere observer. He knew the prophets of the Old Testament; he knew the things they wrought. So he said, "You couldn't do these things You are doing unless God is with You." He wanted to talk to Jesus and get in on the thing and understand what He was doing. So Jesus said a very significant thing. "There's no use for me to try to teach you. You wouldn't know what I'm talking about. You couldn't understand what I'm saying. You'll have to qualify for being enrolled in this institution. You'll have to have certain grades. We can't take you on the training you've had. You'll have to start all over again. If you're going to get these spiritual things I'm talking about, you'll have to be born a second time. 'Except a man be born again, he cannot see the kingdom of God' " (John 3:3). That's what Jesus said in substance. He wouldn't matriculate in His institution a scholar and a gentleman and a religionist who hadn't been born a second time.

Isn't it strange that people talk about being naturally a Christian—you're not naturally a Christian. You're naturally a sinner. "All have sinned, and come short of the glory of God" (Romans 3:23).

There's a word in every vocabulary in the world and every dialect in the world that means "duty" or "must." There's a sense of obligation in the hearts of all people, and there's a feeling and a realization that everybody's done wrong. Everyone has a consciousness that he needs something that he doesn't have naturally.

Born from on high

That's what Jesus is talking about here. He's talking about a new birth, a new nature, a new life, and that comes to us when we are born a second time.

I had a very interesting letter one time from a young fellow who wanted to enroll in our school. You know, with the type of institution we have, we have to be very careful, because some mothers who have bad sons will say, "We'll send him down to Bob Jones University, and Bob Jones University will straighten him out." That's a great compliment to the school, but that woman has the wrong conception of this school.

So we had this letter from a fellow who wanted to come here, and we asked somebody about him and found out that the boy had been in jail four or five times. We were told, "He hasn't done many very bad things. It's true he did steal one automobile, and he did try to kill a fellow and got in jail for it, but he isn't such a bad fellow. If you'd just get him down there, you could fix him."

I said, "Bob Jones University is not a reformatory. A Christian educational institution is not a reformatory. I'm an evangelist. When I go out as an evangelist, murderers and drunkards and thieves are converted. My business as an evangelist is to get folks converted. But our job in Bob Jones University is to train *born-again* Christians so they'll be Christian leaders. That's our purpose. Certainly, if a fellow comes here unsaved, we try to get him converted. But you know, it's rather interesting how people think of

"My friends"

a school as a reformatory."

And one woman wrote us one of the meanest letters you ever read because we wouldn't take her son who was a terrible sinner and help her bring him up right. Well, we said, "My dear woman, he couldn't have got in the school that Jesus Christ founded. Don't jump on us and say we're not Christlike. Christ refused to talk to a man who hadn't been born again because 'You won't know what I'm talking about; I can't matriculate you until you are born again.'"

Listen, men and women, you can't be a Christian until you are born again. You cannot get a Christian education until you are first a Christian. You can get a religious education, you can be taught what the Bible says, "The things of the Spirit of God ... are spiritually discerned" (I Corinthians 2:14). You can't comprehend the spiritual unless you are born again.

One of the most significant things ever uttered was uttered by a prophet in the Old Testament. That prophet was Elijah. He and Elisha were walking along, and Elijah knew he was going to be translated. As they were going along together, Elisha said, "I pray thee, let a double portion of thy spirit be upon me" (II Kings 2:9). "You know, Elijah, I'd like to wear your robe. I'd like to be a prophet; I'd like to be the head of the school when you're gone." And Elijah said, "If thou see me when I am taken from thee, it shall be so unto thee" (verse 10). In other words, he said, "I'm going to be supernaturally translated; if you can comprehend the supernatural, you can

Born from on high

wear a prophet's robe."

No man can wear a prophet's robe who cannot comprehend the supernatural. The saddest thing in the world is a preacher who isn't a born-again man. Next to that, the saddest thing I know is an official church member who has never been born again running a church. And we tell our students in Bob Jones University, "The first essential to a Christian education is to get a new nature, to be regenerated, to become a Christian. And if you're born again, you are a Christian; if you are not born again, you are not a Christian." That's what Jesus said.

You can be born again. "As many as received him, to them gave He power to become the sons of God, even to them that believe on his name" (John 1:12). Why don't you accept Him as your Saviour?

Our Father, we pray for somebody who may have read this message that doesn't know Christ—somebody who has never been born again. Help him or her to yield to Jesus Christ, and definitely, and in simple faith, trust the Lord Jesus Christ as Saviour. Make us faithful and true to Thee. We pray in the name of the Lord Jesus. Amen.

"God is the same person yesterday, today, and forever; but in the drama of the ages He plays many parts."

My friends, the saying that I have just given you is a statement that we need to think a great deal about in the day in which we are living. People have such strange ideas about God and so often misunderstand God because they do not realize the truth of this statement.

You know, in Bob Jones University, we give music and speech and all the arts without any additional cost above academic tuition. We put a great deal of emphasis on speech because we think it makes good show-window material for the Lord Jesus Christ. If a preacher's going to preach, he needs speech. If a young woman is going to teach school, she needs speech. If she's going to be a secretary, it's nice for her to have speech. It does something for her. So we emphasize speech and music. Well, one day I passed the department of speech studios and I heard the head of the department say, "Now, stay

"My friends"

in character. Stay in character. You're not in character in that part." And I got to thinking about it. That's clear, isn't it? If an actor is in character, he's at his best. If it's comedy, he isn't to cry when he's playing comedy—he's to be pleasant. It's a laughing mood, see? And if it's tragedy and he's crying, he certainly isn't supposed to have a lot of fun—he's to stay in character.

I read in the paper some time ago where some actor had many roles he'd taken—numbers and numbers of parts he'd played on the stage. Well, it gave me an idea for this message. Here was an actor, he'd lived his life and had taken the place of one character in this drama and then in another play another character, but he was always the same actor.

Now God is the same yesterday and today and forever. He never changes. He's just, He's holy, He's good, He's everything that you've ever heard and everything you've ever read and more than you can think. But God appears in the drama of the ages in different characters.

You go back into the distant past, and the first picture you have of God is in the character of the Creator. He strikes a match on the rock of omnipotence and begins to light suns and make worlds. And you say, "He's a great Creator." You see Him planting a garden and the first thing you know He is making a man and then giving that man a wife, because the man is lonely.

And then you see God come into the Garden of Eden visiting His friend Adam, and calling on

God is always the same

him and walking with him. There He is in the character of a neighbor and a friend, sympathetic and understanding.

Then you see God in the character of the head of government. He's the ruler of this universe, and He tells man what to do and what not to do. And God in that character doesn't tolerate disobedience. Adam and Eve sinned and God cast them out of the Garden, even though He loved them. He said, "I am going to prepare a plan of redemption for them." He is a just ruler, and He measured out the penalty. He would not have justice tampered with.

Time passes and the first thing you know, God is up in Heaven, and blood is crying up from the earth. There is the blood of Abel, and God Almighty says, "I can't stand that sort of thing—brother killing brother." And then you see God coming to Cain and saying to him, "Now Cain, I'm going to protect you, but you're going to be marked—you can't get away with your sin." There's a God of justice.

Then we move into the New Testament. A baby is born in Bethlehem, a baby who would later say, "You've seen me, you've seen the Father. I am God." A young ruler came to Him and said, "Good Master." And Christ responded, "What are you calling me good for? If I'm not God, I'm not good. I'm an imposter if I'm not God. I'm God."

And then you see Jesus Christ as the Son of God. All power is given to Him, in Heaven and in earth. He opens the door of the day; He pulls

"My friends"

down the shade in the evening: the stars move at His command.

And yet there He is walking around among men. He lets folks spit in His face; He lets them shove Him around. He's in the character of a servant—meek and lowly. Instead of riding down the highway of time in a chariot, He rides a donkey. He's our king in the role of a sinner. And then after a while you see Him, as He hangs on a cross, bloody and mangled and dead. He laid His life down. Then you see Him buried in a tomb. Then He comes up from the dead. You see Him now in the character of a conqueror, for He laid down His life and took it again.

After a while, you see Him going back up on high and playing another role. He's seated at the right hand of the Father, up there in Heaven. And you watch Him there. He knows everything is coming out all right. He's in the role of a contented person who's done what He is supposed to do and knows how things are going to work out.

Now wait a minute. The world has a wrong idea of God. So many people think God will take just anything. He won't. The Christ who came and played the part of a servant—a lowly one, a suffering one—and died on the cross is God's King. He is an heir to all things. And when we turn the telescope of prophecy to the future in the book of Revelation, we see Jesus Christ coming out of Heaven, armed for battle, and riding a white charger. There's an army coming behind Him; His sword is in His mouth; they're a-

God is always the same

marching on. Say, God won't stand everything. Let's not get the wrong idea of God. Nobody will spit in the face of Jesus Christ when He comes back next time. The door of mercy's open now, but the day of justice is coming. And the most startling word in all the Bible is, "The great day of his wrath is come; and who shall be able to stand?" (Revelation 6:17).

A great preacher said, "It looks like God is getting ready to finish up this old world." We tell our students in Bob Jones University that God Almighty never lets anybody get away with wrongdoing, that there's one game that nobody can beat. No human being was ever big enough and wise enough and shrewd enough and enough of a genius to do wrong and get away with it. You must never presume on the mercy of God. And don't you figure too much about Jesus Christ being merciful and kind—He is; He's all that. But He's also just, and you've got to look into His face someday. You'd better quit playing with eternity and judgment and come clean with Him. The Spirit of God is speaking to some of your hearts, and you'd better yield your life to Him and surrender to Him. You've got the opportunity to do it. They used to say, "While the light holds out to burn, the vilest sinner may return."

Our Heavenly Father, hear us for those who are not right, and for those who are right. Help us to think straight, to think clearly about God, to have the right attitude toward sin and the right attitude toward God's holiness. We thank Thee for

"My friends"

His mercy and His love and His saving grace. Keep us true to Him, we pray in His name. Amen.

"Your character is what God knows you to be; your reputation is what men think you are."

My friends, I want to talk to you on the subject of character and reputation, not from the standpoint of men being strong or men being weak but from a moral standpoint.

You hear people talk about how to make and hold friends. That's fine. But sometimes there's a tendency to overdo this friendship business. You're not to make friends at any price. You had better be friendless and be right, than have many friends and be wrong.

Jesus Christ was "despised and rejected of men" (Isaiah 53:3). He was cast out by the religious leaders of His day. He was spurned and rejected. And He had no reputation except among the few people He had blessed. He died that terrible death on the cross. His reputation wasn't very good with some people. They accused Him of everything in the world. They said He wasn't a friend of Caesar's and that He was in

"My friends"

business with the Devil. They said that He was a partner of Satan himself. They even said He was conceived out of wedlock. He was maligned and slandered and misrepresented and misunderstood. "He came unto his own, and his own received him not" (John 1:11). And yet He who was sinless and spotless and clean and noble and courageous—He who never compromised—went up on the hilltop and died on that cross. He had no reputation, but in the sight of God, He was spotless; He was the spotless Lamb of God.

Some people in this world go along and make up with everybody. I've been preaching a long time, but I've never had my business jammed in dealing with the public. God's been good to me. I've never had to stand on a platform and retract a statement I've ever made. I've stood on a few fundamental principles that I believe are essential to character and essential to loyalty to Jesus Christ and the Gospel. I've never tried to make up with everybody. I know I can't be a friend of God and have everybody in the world for me. The world (the organized world, the world system) put the Saviour of the world on the cross, and if I take His side, I can't expect everybody to be for me. This organized world system has on its hands the blood of the Son of God. This world, as the song goes, is no friend to grace to help me on to God.

Only a minority of the people in the world claim to be Christians. There are teeming millions of people in the Orient, and only a small percentage of them are Christians. And you know, in

Character and reputation

countries that we call Christian countries, multitudes of people are not Christians. We speak of America as a Christian nation, but this isn't a Christian nation. Now don't misunderstand me, every good thing we have comes from Christianity and God and the Bible, and we'd be in a terrible fix if there had been no Christian rights in this country. But this isn't a Christian nation. You can't read the stories that come out of Washington and the stories that come out of the state capitals and call this a Christian nation. You can't read of all the crimes being committed or of the influence of the underworld, or the political groups that march to the polls and vote selfishly without any regard for the country or the welfare of people as a whole, and call this a Christian country. You can't see these empty churches and call it a Christian nation. It isn't a Christian nation. We have everything good from Christianity, but there is no Christian nation in the world. If this were a Christian nation, Jesus Christ would have first place, and He hasn't got first place.

A great many people have the reputation of being Christians who are not Christians. But God knows who's who. "The Lord knoweth them that are his." And He said, "Let every one that nameth the name of Christ depart from iniquity" (II Timothy 2:19).

Now, what are you? Don't dodge the issue. I didn't ask, "What do men think you are?" There's a big difference between what men are sometimes and what people think they are.

"My friends"

Sometimes there's a big difference between what a man is and what his wife thinks he is. I wonder, if your wife knew you like God knows you, if her heart wouldn't break.

And what about you as a wife? I was brought up to have the utmost respect for women. When I was a boy, there were no scandals connected with the name of any woman anywhere near my home. But I'll never forget the shock that came to me when I got out into the world and began to preach the Gospel. The most terrible confessions I've ever heard fall from human lips have been the confessions of women, some of whom were supposed to be pure and decent. They said, "You know, I really think I'm going to Hell; I've been so bad."

If all the skeletons in all the closets of all the people reading this were brought out and dangled in the faces of the teeming millions who are going to assemble at the judgment bar of God, God wouldn't have to tell people to go to Hell; they'd just go to Hell anyhow. He wouldn't have to say, "Depart." You'd look at God and listen to the rattling of the skeletons and you'd turn your back on God and your face toward Hell and say, "I ought to go to Hell."

I've had men and women say, "I ought to go to Hell. People think I'm decent, but look at me." A woman said to me once, "I never had any special conviction for sin till now. I didn't know about sin being such an awful thing. But here I am, a poor miserable sinner. I have two sweet babies. And my good husband thinks I'm the best woman in

Character and reputation

the world. I deserve to die and go to Hell."

Say, men and women, what your neighbor thinks you are is your reputation, but what God knows you are—that's your character. (You may be weak in some ways, you may lack force of character, but I'm talking about moral quality now.) You young people, what are you in the sight of a holy God? I didn't ask what do your mother and dad think.

I read some time ago in the paper where one third of a graduating class of a high school went out in the park and had a drunken party, called a "sneak party," and they got drunk. Whiskey was distributed around by some of the athletes of the school.

Now, the moral conditions of this nation are growing worse every day. Let me tell you something; we're going to settle with God Almighty some of these days. In the old days, we had standards in America. And at Bob Jones University we have the hardest time selling our moral standards to the public. "Why," they say, "I wouldn't go there to that school. You have some discipline in that school." That's a reflection, not on Bob Jones University, but a reflection on the age in which we are living. When I was a boy, we *expected* discipline and standards. In all these years at Bob Jones University, we've never had a serious scandal. We've kept our standards through the years, and we're not going to surrender those standards. Come what may, we're going to keep those standards high.

Character is what *God* knows us to be, and

"My friends"

reputation is what men think we are. We're going to keep our character, the character of our institution, and some day all of us are going to answer to God and we'd better be right.

Oh Lord God, help somebody that's living in sin to start all over again and turn to the forgiving mercy of God. For some day we've got to look into Thy face, and it'll be a terrible day for people unless they are saved by the grace of God. Then help us all to live for Thee and be from now on what we ought to be. We pray in the name of the Lord Jesus. Amen.

"A Christian does good deeds, but doing good deeds does not make a man a Christian."

My friends, in my many years of evangelistic work, I think two of the most difficult things I've had to do is convince people that they're either saved or lost, and that they cannot save themselves.

It's a strange thing; way down in his heart, the average man has a feeling that he can, by some good deed, save himself. He has the idea that, up in Heaven, the angels are bookkeepers, and when he does a good deed, an angel puts it in one column, and when he does a bad deed, an angel puts that deed in another column. And he has a feeling that, when he dies, the angels will add up those columns, and if the good is bigger than the bad, he goes to Heaven; and if the bad is bigger than the good, he goes to Hell.

Some people think that education or charity or being kind to people can save. I don't see where they get such an idea. Eternity's a long

"My friends"

time, and Heaven, according to the Bible, is a wonderful place. Think of a man having little enough sense to believe that he can stay in this world just a few years and can do a little good while he's down here, and then, when he dies, live in Heaven forever, have a beautiful home, a lovely room, never have any sickness or sorrow, no sighing, no crying, no dying, forever and forever—and he can buy all that with just some good little thing that he might do in this world! A fellow who thinks that just doesn't have ordinary, common, everyday, practical business sense. Salvation is something that is so priceless that the Lord Jesus Christ, God's Son, had to buy it with His own precious blood. He came down from Heaven, went to Calvary's cross and died that men might be saved.

If men are saved, they will do good deeds; and yet doing good deeds will not save men. A man has to be good to do the right kind of good deeds. A deed is not a good deed that's not done for the glory of God. We read in the Bible, "though I give my body to be burned," and though I do a thousand other things, "and have not charity, it profiteth me nothing" (I Corinthians 13:3). It may do somebody else some good. You might give some money to missions, and send the missionary out to the foreign field, and still be an old sinner. Your money might buy a ticket across the ocean for the missionary, and the missionary might do somebody some good in some foreign field; but giving your money to that missionary won't do you one bit of good as far as your salvation is con-

Christians and good deeds

cerned. And it will not give you any reward in time or eternity unless you did it because you love God and want to do what's right.

As a preacher of the Gospel, I find it very difficult to get this idea over to people. I meet a man and say to him, "Are you a Christian?" and he says, "Well, I do about the best I can." I meet somebody else, and he says, "I think I'm about as good as some church members."

In the Bible classes at Bob Jones University, we teach our students that men are not saved by what they do, but are saved by accepting what the Lord Jesus Christ has done for them. We drill that especially into our ministerial students and, of course, our missionary students.

A good many of our students at Bob Jones University are preparing for the ministry and for the foreign mission field, though our university is no more of a preacher's school or a missionary's school than it is a teacher's school, or a school of science, or a school of language, or some other kind of school. When we maintain the Christian emphasis that we do in Bob Jones University, young men who want to study for the ministry and young folks who hope to be missionaries gravitate to the school.

People are always putting on a campaign to get preachers, and churches say, "We've got to have a lot of preachers." Well, I'll tell you how to get all the preachers you want and all the Christian workers you need. Just run a good Christian school! Or have a good Christian Sunday school, or a good Christian church. Put

"My friends"

the emphasis in the right place; and if you put the emphasis in the right place, God takes care of everything else for you.

So at Bob Jones University we tell our girls, if you're going to be a housekeeper, and that's what God wants you to do, that's just as sacred as being a missionary. "Life's not divided into the secular and the sacred—everything's sacred for a Christian." But whether a girl is going to marry and keep house, or whether a boy is going to be a preacher or lawyer or a doctor or a teacher or a businessman or whatever he's going to be, we tell our students that as Christian people, their first obligation is to Almighty God, and that all of them ought to go out to give a Christian testimony. Then we try to explain to them what a Christian testimony is.

Here is the Gospel: Jesus Christ "died for our sins according to the Scriptures; And that he was buried, and that he rose again the third day according to the Scriptures" (ICorinthians 15:3, 4). Men are saved by trusting Jesus Christ; they cannot save themselves; they cannot earn salvation; they cannot pay for it after they get it. If you lived a million years on this earth, and never did any harm, and did good every day you lived, these good deeds you do cannot take you to Heaven when you die. And if you're counting on your good deeds to save you, you have no conception of the real plan of salvation and the real value of being saved.

One time I saw an old-time preacher die, and he was a wonderful man. And while he was

Christians and good deeds

dying, I stood by his bed. His son, who was a minister, got down on his knees and said, "Father, let your mantle fall on me."

And the old man said, "Son, get the mantle of the Lord. My mantle is in rags and tatters."

But the son said, "Oh father, look how much good you've done. You've been preaching for 50 years."

And the old man said, "Don't tell me that, son. Tell me about the blood of Jesus. Nothing but the blood of Jesus can save a dying man."

Well, he was right. You can't save yourself. You can't earn salvation. All the good deeds that you do—and you will do good deeds if you're a decent man or a decent woman—they'll not save you.

The right kind of good deeds are the fruit that grows on the tree of a real Christian experience. A man who is good as he ought to be, will do good deeds; and he'll do what he does for the glory of God. That's the standard. "Whatsoever ye do, do all to the glory of God" (I Corinthians 10:31). Our business as Christians is to exalt Jesus Christ— lift Him up, magnify Him, exalt Him to the right place in our thinking and in our testimony. We should magnify the name of the Lord Jesus Christ. Now if you're right, you will do that.

Some people are mighty nice and are not Christians. I know some people who are lovely, courteous, kind, friendly—and you love people like that. But when you trust your good deeds to save you, you're not saved. The gentlest thing I ever saw was a little dog I had when I was a boy.

"My friends"

Dogs can be affectionate, horses can be gentle, but they can't be Christians. And you can be gentle and kind and do many lovely things, but doing these things will not save you.

But if you want to be saved, you can be saved. Jesus said, "Him that cometh to me I will in no wise cast out" (John 6:37). You can come to Him if you wish to; His arms are open wide, and He'll take you.

Our Father, help somebody who reads these words to come to Jesus and trust Him as his Saviour; and may we meet somebody in Heaven because of this little, simple message. We pray in the name of the Lord Jesus. Amen.

> *"An illiterate person is one who cannot tell you what he knows; an ignorant person is one who does not know anything to tell you."*

My friends, as I've gone up and down this country and have travelled in other lands preaching the Gospel of God's saving grace, I have met a great many people who seem to feel that the trouble with the world is a lack of education.

Ignorance is not the trouble with the world. You can be illiterate and still not be ignorant. And you can be literate and still be ignorant. I've met some Ph.D's that needed to sit at the feet of some illiterates that I have known. For instance, if you don't know God, you don't know the main thing that's to be known. The Bible says, "The fear of the Lord is the beginning of knowledge" (Proverbs 1:7). The literal meaning is that the fear of God is a chief part of knowledge. The word "fear" here is that sort of fear that means reverence for God, the recognition of God, giving God His proper place in our thinking, the exaltation of God to His place in the universe in

"My friends"

our thinking. That's what it means by "the fear of the Lord."

You can take me in the laboratory and tell me things that I do not know about the universe. You can be a great scholar. But, in the truest sense, a man knows more that's worth knowing if he knows God made this universe than a man who knows a great deal about the universe. You can know music without knowing God. You can know astronomy without knowing God. "The heavens declare the glory of God; and the firmament sheweth his handiwork" (Psalm 19:1). You can say, "There must have been a great cause somewhere." But you have no special reverence for that cause, and you do not worship that great cause—you do not worship God.

All of your scholarship doesn't make you a man to be depended upon if you do not know God. For my philosophy of life, I'd rather sit in a mountain cabin somewhere at the feet of a woman who can scarcely read but who knows God than to sit at the feet of the greatest scholar the world ever saw, unless that scholar knows God. "The world by wisdom knew not God" (I Corinthians 1:21).

We come to know God by faith. *Faith!* Oh, you say you don't believe in faith, but you do. You learned your alphabet by faith. You went to school and the teacher said, "This is 'A,' " and you said, "That's 'A' "; the teacher said, "This is 'B,' " and you said, "That's 'B.' " You took a teacher's word for your alphabet. You know now the teacher was right.

Illiteracy and ignorance

When I was a country boy, I learned my divine alphabet by faith. My mother said, "Jesus was the Son of God. He died on the cross to save people. He rose again from the dead." My father said the same thing. I'd go around to country churches and they'd have what they called "experience meetings," and somebody would get up and say, "I was a drunkard and tried to quit whiskey. I was an awful sinner, mean to my wife, and I blasphemed the name of God. But one day I trusted Jesus, and He fixed me up and He delivered me from drink. He set me free. Jesus is so wonderful to me." Everywhere I went people were saying that.

Paul told about going down the Damascus road and how Jesus spoke to him from Heaven on that highway. Paul's life was changed. Before that time, Paul would kill everybody who didn't agree with him, and now he was willing to die for the cause he represented.

I said, "Well, I believe I'll try this thing out." So I turned myself over to Jesus Christ and trusted Him as my Saviour. I know He's the Son of God. Nobody but the Son of God could do for me what Jesus Christ had done. And nobody but the Son of God can do what I've seen Jesus Christ do for men and women all over the world. Now, we tell our students, "You can learn mathematics, you can learn science, you get all your lessons, but if you don't know God, you don't know the real thing that you ought to know." And if a student happens to come to Bob Jones University unsaved, the first thing we try to do is

"My friends"

to win him to Jesus Christ.

A Christian school is not a Christian school unless it puts the first emphasis upon knowing God. That's the first emphasis. When you put the emphasis anywhere else except on knowing God, you do not have a Christian school. You may have a good scientific laboratory, you may have a very fine library—and those things are all right; a school that's a Christian school *will* have a good library, it *will* have a good laboratory, it *will* have the best of everything it can have. Everything else being equal, a Christian school will keep its buildings better than a school that isn't Christian. We tell our students at Bob Jones University that these buildings belong to God. They don't scratch up the walls, and you don't find anybody on our campus destroying property.

Christianity doesn't make people inefficient; it makes them efficient. It makes them produce; it makes them deliver; it makes them do everything better. It makes a man a better husband. It makes a woman a better wife. It makes parents better parents. It makes children better children. It makes a better businessman. There isn't a businessman who's running a legitimate business who couldn't do it better if he were a Christian. Knowing God is the main thing in life. If you don't know God, you don't know anything that's worth knowing, because all the other knowledge that you have will pass away when you die. You'll be taken out to the cemetery and put to bed with a shovel and covered up with dirt. But your immortal spirit lives on and on, and God lives on

Illiteracy and ignorance

and on, and you will live as long as God lives.

You can know God. Paul said, "I know whom I have believed" (II Timothy 1:12) (not *in* whom—that's not the best rendering); "I know *whom* I have believed." You know, we've been subnormal spiritually in this country so long. If an educational institution or even a church gets to be really normal, people think the institution or the church is running a high temperature. You put the first emphasis on God—that's what makes a Christian school; that's what makes a Christian church. It isn't just teaching mathematics—you can learn mathematics and die some day and go to Hell. You can learn science and be lost forever. But knowing God is the big thing, and I wonder if you know Him. I didn't ask you if you were a church member; I'm asking you something else. I'd like to have you face it. Do you know God? Oh, the agnostic says, "I don't know whether there's any God or not." Well, I *do*! I met Him when I was a little boy. He's been with me through the years. I call Him my Father. And God's real to me, and I've met thousands of people to whom God is as real as wife or mother, father, brother, sister, child, friend. He can be real to you. What we need in this country is a real God.

Some people say, "I believe in a first great cause." Well, that's all right, He was back there but you need an up-to-date God, too. You need Somebody who is near you when the hearse backs up to the door, you need Somebody near you when the darkness settles and you don't know what to do. The Bible says wisdom comes from

"My friends"

God. You can acquire knowledge, but what to do with knowledge after you get it—that's wisdom. Wisdom is knowing how to use that knowledge to meet successfully the emergencies of life.

I'm not asking you if you're literate or illiterate—not now—I'm asking you if you are ignorant. I'm asking you if you are ignorant about God and the will of God and the purpose of God and the redeeming grace of God—that's what I'm asking. You can know Him if you want to. He said, "Look unto me, and be ye saved, all the ends of the earth" (Isaiah 45:22). Why don't you come to Him and trust Him? Why don't you yield yourself to Him? God help you to do it.

Our Father, bless somebody who reads this message, somebody who may have been in darkness up until now. Help that someone to look up to the Light. Thou art the Light of the world; Thou art the Light that drives away all the darkness out of the hearts of men. Help people to trust Thee and help us all to be faithful to Thee. And help us to realize that ignorance and illiteracy are not always the same things. Help us to know God, and then if we know Him, we will find a way to tell about Him. Make us faithful to Him, for Jesus' sake. Amen.

"Life is not divided into the secular and the sacred. For a Christian, everything is sacred."

My friends, in my wide experience as a minister of the Gospel and as an evangelist dealing with a mass of people, I have discovered what I consider one of the most serious perils to a real Christian life and Christian testimony. There is an idea abroad that certain things are sacred, and certain things are secular. For instance, some people go to church on Sunday morning, and they walk down the aisle of the church saying, "The Lord is in his holy temple: let all the earth keep silence before him" (Habakkuk 2:20). And then when the service is over, they feel like their sacred job has been done for the day and other things are secular. That isn't so.

God is no more in the church building, or temple, or cathedral than He is anywhere else. God is everywhere. He is an omnipresent God. In the old dispensation, the ancient Israelites used to think it was wonderful that God Who had eter-

"My friends"

nity to inhabit would condescend to dwell in temples made with hands, but in this dispensation God doesn't dwell in temples made with hands. The dwelling place of God in the earth today is in the bodies of people. The Holy Spirit dwells in the bodies of consecrated, surrendered, trusting Christian people. Jesus said it was expedient that He go away, for He said, "If I go not away, the Comforter will not come unto you" (John 16:7).

Now when Jesus was with His disciples, they had wonderful fellowship. And sometimes we envy those disciples who had Jesus with them. But if you are a Christian, you have Jesus in you; the Holy Spirit is the other self of Jesus, and He is in you. The Holy Spirit is just as much God as the Father or the Son. We forget that sometimes. So your body is the temple of the Holy Ghost. Writing to the Corinthians, Paul said, "What? know ye not that your body is the temple of the Holy Ghost which is in you, which ye have of God, and ye are not your own? For ye are bought with a price" (I Corinthians 6:19-20). My body, as a Christian, has in it the Holy Spirit. He that inhabits eternity comes down to earth and dwells in the bodies of men. How wonderfully interesting that is! And yet what a sense of responsibility comes to us when we stop to realize it. Whether you are in the temple, or in the kitchen, or in the automobile riding down the highway when you have a date, if you are a Christian, God is there. We read in the Bible, "Where two or three are gathered together in my name, there

Sacred or secular

am I in the midst of them"—in the midst of them—He is among them (Matthew 18:20). He is *among* the group but *in* every believing Christian.

We've built up a strange idea that when we are here, this is a sacred place. But this place over here is another place, and it doesn't matter much what we do over there. Isn't it strange how crazy we are in our conceptions which are not biblical and not Christian? I believe in keeping the Sabbath—as we say—the Lord's Day. I think it's a shame that we've sacrificed the old-time American Sabbath. When I was a boy, on Sunday we all dressed up and kept that day. We said, "This is God's day." But you know, Sunday is no more God's day than Monday. The church is no more God's house than your home. It's just different. You're not to neglect the assembling of yourselves together, so you go to church to worship God. But at home you serve God too. We are told in the Bible, "Whatsoever ye do, do all to the glory of God" (I Corinthians 10:31). If you are cooking, you are cooking for the glory of God. God has a will about what you cook and how you cook it. God has a will about what you eat. God has a will about how you keep your house. God has a will about the hat you wear and how much you pay for it. God has a will about the sort of clothes you wear.

Everything connected with life is sacred if you're a Christian. Everything is secular with some people, but Christian people should realize that life is not made up into two compartments.

"My friends"

That explains a great many things. It explains why preachers on Sunday morning have a different voice than what they have anywhere else. You meet a preacher and you say, "How are you, Doctor? How are you, Brother So-and-So?" and he says, "Fine, thank you; how are you? Nice to see you." Then a minute later he walks into the pulpit and gets his preacher's voice. He starts out, "Oh, God, our Heavenly Father." He's in another role. Now that accounts for all that. That accounts for the strange, peculiar attitudes that people have that affect their voice. A preacher ought not to have any nicer voice in the pulpit than he has when he's talking to his wife. A soprano in the choir or an alto or anybody else shouldn't have any nicer voice when she sings in the choir than when she talks to her babies at home if she has babies. We ought to use the best voice we have all the time, and we ought not to copy somebody else's voice because we heard somebody else talk a certain way.

Life is wonderful when you think of it in relation to God. I don't know of anything that God is more interested in than the Christian home. Before there was ever a church there was a home—a man and a woman. God said Adam shouldn't be alone; he ought to have some company, so God made him a wife. And God Almighty is interested in the home.

He is interested in your job. He is interested in the kind of work you do. Every year when we open school, we have some student who has to have his idea along this line straightened out. He

Sacred or secular

says, "I'm going to sing now for the Lord." And I say, "You're going to do mathematics for the Lord. You're going to study science for the Lord." Now we won't let students hang around Bob Jones University and stay very long if they think that it isn't as Christian to study as it is to sing or preach. It's just as Christian for a woman to clean up her home in the morning and dress up the babies and fix them up and get them ready for Sunday school as it is for her to take them to Sunday school. All life is sacred if we only stop to realize it.

I remember one time a fellow came into my office and said, "You know, Dr. Bob, I asked the Lord to help me pass my examinations." And I said, "Well, He won't do anything for you." He said, "What do you mean?" I said, "God won't pat you on the back and approve of your laziness. You know God's not that kind of God. You can't be a lazy loafer. You haven't been the student. You haven't studied hard. And do you think that God Almighty will tell you it's all right for you to loaf and He'll come and help you? You're wrong. God doesn't operate that way."

We are supposed to have a God consciousness on every step of the way of life. We read in the Bible, "The plowing of the wicked, is sin" (Proverbs 21:4). But the plowing of a righteous man isn't sin. The plowing of a righteous man, if he's the right kind of righteous man, is plowing for the glory of God. He cultivates God's soil and plows for God. Now people say, "I'm called to preach." I think that's fine, and I believe

"My friends"

in a call to the ministry. Or, "I'm called to be a missionary." That's wonderful, but you women that keep house, we tell our girls in Bob Jones University that most women are called to be married women, have homes, and rear families. God calls most women for that. And if you are where God put you, doing the will of God, your job is just as sacred as the job of a missionary.

The job you have may be far more important than the job that somebody else has that the world thinks is important. I remember a woman one time said, "You know, I used to think when I was a girl I'd like to be a missionary, but circumstances made it impossible for me to be a missionary. I decided if I couldn't, then God didn't want me to be a missionary." She was right. If she couldn't, God didn't want her to. And then she lifted up her little baby and said, "I'm training a missionary. I dedicated my little girl to God to be a missionary." I said, "Well, now, that's fine." It's just as sacred to train a little girl to be a missionary as it is to be a missionary. We built Bob Jones University on this practical foundation. That gives you the little secret of the growth of the school and the practical Christian approach of it, because we put our emphasis there. We put that emphasis wherever we go. Life is not divided into the secular and the sacred. For a Christian, everything in life is sacred. All ground is holy ground, every bush a burning bush, and every place a Christian is, the temple of God is there.

Our Father, bless all who read this message

and pour out Thy Spirit upon them. Help them to be faithful, and let them not be weary in the grinding routine of daily life. But whatever we do in word or deed, help us to do all to the glory of God. We pray in the name of the Lord Jesus. Amen.

"God will not do for you what He gives you strength to do for yourself."

My friends, I told you in the previous message about the student who came into my office one day just before examinations and said, "I've been praying for the Lord to help me pass my examinations." I told him that the Lord was not going to endorse his laziness. That boy was a good boy and came from a very fine Christian home. He believed in prayer and had faith. Those are two wonderful things—prayer and faith. We need to have faith in God and pray. That's all right, and I liked the boy, and I liked his people, but that boy had a wrong slant on his responsibilities.

We read in the Bible, "Study to shew thyself approved unto God." Now, we stand before God as Christians, robed in the righteousness of Jesus Christ; but our own righteousnesses are like "filthy rags." When you came to Jesus, a poor lost sinner, you trusted Jesus as your Saviour, and God robed you with the righteousness of His Son.

"My friends"

That is your standing before God. Timothy was a Christian; he knew the Lord, he was saved, but the Apostle Paul said, "Study, [Timothy,] to shew thyself approved unto God" (II Timothy 2:15). In other words, make an effort. "Approved" is used not in the sense that you're saved—you can't present yourself clean before God as a sinner—but as a Christian you can study. You can make the best preparation possible. You can look into your own heart and into the Word of God and find out what God wants you to do in order to be approved as a child of God and a worker for the Lord Jesus Christ.

Some people have no faith at all. Some people go to an extreme and say, "Well, I don't need anybody to take care of me. I'll take care of myself." I remember one time I was riding on the train and I saw a great big man with a big neck and big shoulders, sitting there smoking a cigar almost as big as he was. We were talking about God and so forth and so on. He said, "You know, I never give anything to any cause or charity of any kind. I started out in the world and I took care of myself. Nobody ever helped me. I made my money—fought my own way along. I'm not obligated to anybody."

I said, "Wait a minute, buddy. You're obligated to God Almighty. Who gave you that chest with those lungs and made you able to breathe? Who pumped the air into your lungs? Who gave you eyesight? I know folks as good as you are, and some of them better, that can't see. I know folks that haven't your chest and your arms and your

Doing things for yourself

health. Here you are talking about not owing anything to anybody."

Every human being is under obligation to God. You may be a sinner and a blasphemer and someday you may die and go to Hell, but you owe God Almighty something. God has been good to you. You never would have seen a flower or a star if it hadn't been for God. You never would have been able to breathe if it hadn't been for God. You owe God a debt of gratitude that some of you have never paid.

We're all obligated to God. Christians are saved because God loved us and Jesus died for us. Now there are some things we can't do for ourselves. We can't save ourselves. All the religions of the world tell men to do and live. The Bible tells men to live and do. As I've said so many times in my ministry, one of the reasons I know the Bible is the Word of God is because I know the mental processes of man. No man would have ever thought of the plan of salvation as outlined in the Bible. Man is always trying to save himself and do something by his own strength and his own power. But one day, some of us saw ourselves as sinners and knew we couldn't save ourselves. We trusted Jesus Christ.

God's not going to do for us Christians what He gives us strength to do for ourselves, and that's in line with the Scripture. You remember where the Bible said if they won't work, don't let them eat (II Thessalonians 3:10). You know, some people want God to be a waiting boy for them. They sit down and press a button and say, "I'd

"My friends"

like to have my breakfast. Send me my food." Now it's all right to pray day by day, "Give us this day our daily bread" (Matthew 6:11). And all the bread that you ever ate came from God. There isn't a crumb of bread that ever fell from a tablecloth that didn't fall first out of the hand of God on that table. But you know, if you don't go in yonder and fix yourself something to eat, God is not going to give it to you. You can do some things God gave you strength to do.

I believe in a practical religion. Bob Jones University emphasizes that and always has emphasized it. I remember one time a fellow came to me and said, "Dr. Bob, I have asked God to send me some money so I can come to college next year." I said, "Why don't you ask God to send you out to get some money? You are able and strong and husky." Now sometimes you can't get any money. Sometimes you're not able to find any money. Sometimes you haven't any strength to go get money. But don't ask God to send you something if you can go get it. God won't do for you what He gives you strength to do for yourself. If you can plow, plow. If you can make a crop, make a crop. If you can earn some money, earn some money. It's perfectly legitimate, perfectly Christian not to ask God to send it to you when you're out and could make it.

I know one fellow that was praying his way through school, and he bought his girl a beautiful diamond while he was praying his way through school. I don't believe in that kind of business—asking God to send you money to go to school and

Doing things for yourself

when God sends you a little extra, you buy a diamond ring for your sweetheart. You ought to have told her to wait for that diamond. She didn't have to have a diamond ring.

I believe in practical religion. I don't believe in wasting money. I've known people in Christian work to waste money. Oh, they were honest good people, but they just threw God's money away. Every day in Bob Jones University we know in advance what a meal is going to cost. If you are feeding three thousand people three times a day, you've got a job on your hands. So a business manager figures out what it's going to cost. We know what it's going to cost us, and then when the day is over, we check to see if it did cost us that much. We think it's a sin to waste God Almighty's money. We believe in practical Christianity, and we need practical Christianity in this country. Oh, I know there's a mystical element in the realm of religion. I know something about the fact that we are citizens of Heaven. We don't belong in this world, but we ought to beat the world at its own game of being practical. Jesus said that "the children of this world are in their generation wiser than the children of light" (Luke 16:8). They are wiser in their generation. They are more practical as far as the knowledge they have of the affairs of things. I've known so many good Christian people who are very impractical. God won't hoe your garden for you. He'll let the weeds take it. God Almighty won't go out and gather you something to eat in the garden. You can go pick the peas yourself. But God steps in

"My friends"

where man doesn't have strength to work, and God sends the sunshine and the rain. God sends the harvest. He does for men what He hasn't given them strength to do for themselves.

You haven't strength to save yourself. You can't buy salvation, you can't pay for it after you get it. There is no way you can qualify by any effort that you can put forth to get a house up in Heaven. But you know what you can do? God steps in here and says, "Look unto me, and be ye saved, all the ends of the earth" (Isaiah 45:22). "I'll save you." "Him that cometh to me I will in no wise cast out" (John 6:37). That's the promise of God. "I will in no wise, under any condition, cast you out if you will come to me." That's God calling you. You can't save yourself. "Believe on the Lord Jesus Christ, and thou shalt be saved" (Acts 16:31). You can believe in the Lord Jesus Christ by the grace of God, but Christ has to save you. But remember the saying, "God will not do for you what He gives you strength to do for yourself."

Our Father, help poor sinners who have read this message to trust you, knowing they cannot save themselves. Then help us Christians to do everything we do in word and deed for the glory of God. Help us according to divine injunction to be diligent in business, and at the same time, fervent in spirit, serving the Lord. Hear us in this prayer and keep us faithful and true to Thee and lead us by Thy Spirit in the way Thou wouldst have us go. We pray in the name of the Lord Jesus. Amen.

"The wise man prepares for the inevitable."

My friends, as I have gone about the world preaching the Gospel and dealing with people about their souls, I have found that, so many times when you think people have good sense, they didn't have good sense. Some people who thought they were very smart were so impractical. If a man isn't practical, he hasn't good sense. He may be a great musician, be talented, be gifted, and be able to do something in certain realms and achieve in a certain way, but a man who does not know how to adjust his talents to the practical things of life is not a balanced man.

One of the things that we emphasize in Bob Jones University is this: if a thing hasn't got sense in it, God isn't in it. We are in this world. We're not in Heaven yet. We believe in the "sweet bye and bye" but we are in the nasty now and now. We're down here in a dirty world of sin and shame where we've got to live until we leave it.

"My friends"

We're here, and God Almighty steps in and offers to take care of us while we are here, but we're in a world.

The world itself isn't practical, and there are very few practical people. This little saying, "The wise man prepares for the inevitable," would solve all the problems of life. There are some things that men do not know how to prepare for. Sometimes the world changes and governments change. Sometimes the value of money changes and sometimes there are things that happen to us. You may go out and cultivate your land and do a good job in sowing the seed, but there may be a disaster such as an earthquake, or a storm, or a drought. You may not make a crop. There are some things that men do not know how to prepare for, but the man who is properly related to God Almighty is prepared whatever happens. You're prepared for whatever comes in this world if your relation to God is right.

I remember just as World War I was closing. I was talking to a relative of mine who is a very practical sort of fellow. He was not what you'd call aggressively spiritual, but he was a Christian at heart. So I said to him one day, "Have you read this article by a group of British preachers to the effect that this is probably the beginning of the close of the age in which we are living?" Many Bible scholars believe with World War I we began to reach the end of the age and that we are living now in what might be called the last act of the great tragedy of human life on this earth. In the next act, when the curtain goes

Preparing to die

down, the age may end. Things point that way. Jesus, in the sermon on the Mount of Olives, said that Jerusalem should be "trodden down of the Gentiles, until the times of the Gentiles be fulfilled" (Luke 21:24); and Jerusalem has been trodden down of the Gentiles for more than 2000 years. Now there's a government of Israel.

As I was talking to this relative of mine about these things, I said to him, "Now, I want to know if you're saved. I want to know if you're a Christian—if you're right with God. You and I don't know what's going to happen, but if the Lord comes quickly, I want you to be ready." He looked at me and said something I have never forgotten. He said, "Bob, I don't know what's going to happen, but I'm trusting Jesus Christ and I'll be ready whatever happens."

The only man who is ready for the inevitable is the man who is properly related to God Almighty. He is ready whatever comes. If you are in harmony with His will, trusting Jesus Christ as your Saviour, and surrendered to Him, you are ready whatever may come. You may die; you may die sooner than you think; but you are ready if you are rightly related to Christ, if He's your Saviour. People talk about deathbed stories and about evangelists' preaching along that line. Did you ever stop to think, the man who is ready to die any moment is a mighty good man to have around in this world? A fellow who is ready for death, the inevitable, is a mighty fine fellow; so the best preparation that you can make for this life, the best preparation you can make as a hus-

"My friends"

band or wife, father or mother, son or daughter, businessman, or professional man is to be prepared for eternity.

I get so sick of these people who think you're not practical if you are a Christian. They think you're impractical. There are people in this country who think because Bob Jones University puts the first emphasis on the Lord Jesus Christ and Christian experience and a young person being properly related to God that we are a bunch of fanatics! Why, there's no fanaticism on our campus. We are practical, intelligent, commonsense, everyday normal people. We have culture; we give music and speech without any additional cost above academic tuition. We teach our young preachers to be practical out in their ministry. But no man is a wise man who isn't prepared for the inevitable.

One time a prominent businessman said to me, "Well now, Dr. Bob, of course, we all think a great deal of you, but you're a preacher and you, of course, are not a businessman, and you can't see things from the standpoint of a businessman." I said, "Don't talk to me like that. You businessmen have made a mess of the world. I don't see how anybody struts his stuff in this world in which we are living. Nations have come up and gone down. The dust of the centuries blows over the bones of buried civilizations. And here you are talking wise. What do you know? What does anybody know?"

The man who is prepared for eternity is also prepared for time. And the man who is prepared

Preparing to die

for whatever may come is prepared for the inevitable because he is properly related to Jesus Christ. We tell our students at Bob Jones University, "If you don't get properly related to God and to Jesus Christ, His Son, as your Saviour, and properly related to eternal values, you'll not be adjusted to the values that are here now." A man cannot have the right slant on temporal values who doesn't first get the right slant on spiritual values. That which is seen is temporal; that which is unseen is eternal. There isn't any temporal value that has value unless it has spiritual value tied up with it.

I'm a practical person and I'd like to ask you how, as a practical person, are you prepared for whatever happens—death, eternity, judgment? You'd better be and you can be. You can trust Jesus Christ as your Saviour, become a Christian, and relate yourself to all that is inevitable and be ready for anything that happens.

Our Father, help us not to be wise in our own estimation of wisdom. Give us the wisdom from above, not the wisdom of the world. It seems to fail everybody, but the wisdom from above is eternal. Give it to us so we may be prepared for whatever may come to us. And keep us faithful in everything. We pray in the name of the Lord Jesus Christ, our Saviour. Amen.